THE SONG AND THE SWALLOW

Authenticity
and Love

MATTHEW ANGHELOS MARCH

FriesenPress

One Printers Way
Altona, MB R0G 0B0
Canada

www.friesenpress.com

Copyright © 2022 by Matthew Anghelos March
First Edition — 2022

Cover Art by Brady Sato

ISBN
978-1-03-913627-4 (Hardcover)
978-1-03-913626-7 (Paperback)
978-1-03-913628-1 (eBook)

1. PHILOSOPHY, SOCIAL

Distributed to the trade by The Ingram Book Company

For my mother,
who has a heart and sharp teeth,
but no maw to speak of.

A

DOUBT THYSELF

———

To anticipate which things will change your life is impossible, a truth with which many of us have become familiar, despite a desire to combat the unexpected. Some things resonate with us in such an impactful way, our instincts tell us that it must be a potent abstraction untethered from reality. How could something earthly be so powerful? Sometimes though, life-changing events are guided by real things, and this can often magnify its effect on us; the tangibility of it providing us with a sense of hope in pursuing the journey that may be calling out to us. We can be additionally fortunate if we are capable of recalling exactly the details of these events, the specificity of them providing insight into our tendencies and apprehensions. I recall one of these events for me, and it is one that I consider myself fortunate in having experienced in my late teens, at a time when we all fantasize about having a forbidden truth revealed to us.

This event took place in a high school philosophy class. According to my teacher, in ancient Greece the Temple of Apollo stood at Delphi, on the south-western slope of Mount Parnassus. Only the ruins remain today, but at one time it was commonplace for anyone desiring assistance with or insight into important issues to seek consultation with the oracle who operated there, which was the Pythia, or high priestess of the temple. Inscriptions were commonplace in ancient Greek architecture, and one of the maxims present in the forecourt of the temple translates to "know thyself." Peculiar, isn't it? I imagined people travelling from all over Greece to see the oracle and encountering aphorisms pedantically recommending to them to *know themselves*, whatever is being insinuated by this. It was after this brief thought, which came swiftly, as most conclusions do in the mind of a young adult, that I considered its implications. Know myself? As if I don't already? How is it that something so stupid came to be inscribed on the temple of a clairvoyant? I mean, *she should've been able to predict that's stupid*, I jokingly thought to myself. Maybe she's just young and beautiful, or she's willing to perform sexual favours with patrons in order to *maximize her prophetic abilities*, and that's what the fuss is all about. I was far more cynical in my youth, what can I say?

Since this was a philosophy class, I figured that maybe I should spend some time actually considering it as a plausible recommendation. I'll suspend my judgment for now, and adopt a philosophical approach; after all, learning how to think differently is the point of education, is it not? If I were to assume that making a concerted effort to think differently was a waste of time, then I would be essentially implying that I know the best way to think already, and that it cannot be improved upon, which I felt was an obvious dictation of my ego and a dismissal of human progress. Let's suppose that I don't innately know myself; this would have to be due to one of four possible reasons, or so I decided at the time:

1. Humans do not innately possess the ability to self-examine to the point of obtaining reliable self-knowledge.

2. Humans possess the ability to obtain self-knowledge, but we cannot properly pursue it due to some factor that impedes this, but the impediment is not that we lack the ability.

3. Humans possess the ability to obtain self-knowledge, but we don't find it advantageous to do so and as a result we may not engage in this pursuit for whatever reason.

4. Humans possess the ability to self-examine to the point of self-knowledge, but I personally lack the requisite abilities and desires to do so because of an anomalous reason of which I am unaware.

After much consideration, I came to a horrifying conclusion: I had no idea which one of these was the case. Where do you even start with this sort of problem? I started to realize very quickly that even if there was a solution to this problem, I certainly didn't possess the knowledge or the ability necessary to discover it. So then, I had a choice to make, I could either just accept that this wasn't worth pursuing, or I could see if it was possible to obtain the knowledge necessary to tackle it. This isn't much of a choice really; the issue pertains to knowing yourself, and I imagined what the trajectory of my life would be if I persisted in my potential ignorance of myself. How can I be honest about anything if I don't know myself? What if the decisions I make are based on things I believe to be true about myself but aren't? What if I end up in a career I hate because my choice was based on what I *thought* my interests and desires are? Am I going to be willing to change my life at any point if I'm not nearly as courageous as I'd like to think I am? And if not, how do I recognize my cowardice, and understand the cause of it and how to overcome it so I can become courageous?

Then the most important question of all hit me, in the mixture of odd thoughts and hyperbole: *what do I even know about myself?* This may seem a little exaggerated, but I was deadly serious about it. To think you know yourself, and to truly know aren't the same thing at all. What exactly about my mind and my body did I really know? Certainly, information isn't knowledge, and facts are claims about reality, but they could be either true or false. How much of what I thought I knew constituted actual knowledge, and how might I reliably distinguish the difference? My world unravelled, but only for an instant. Counterintuitively, I felt more alive than I ever had before. I was energized by the devastating doubt thrust upon my psyche, and I instinctively pushed back up against it to meet its challenge and wrestle it into submission so it may not escape. I recognize this isn't the case for most people. Doubt is a complicated thing, and it earns more than its fair share of negative attention.

Tipping the Scales

Doubt is many things. It is a looming sense of insecurity when you're competing athletically, or about to deliver a presentation at school or at work, or wondering whether someone will be as interested as you are to go on a date. It is dangerous when stressful situations present themselves and panic begins to arise in you and you start to question your ability to do CPR on your loved one who just collapsed in front of you, or you wonder whether you're really doing the right thing when you engage in combat as a soldier. It is weakness when

4

you're an alleged expert or leader and you don't want to bear the possibility that you may have done something wrong. These are all real experiences that we may encounter at some point, but doubt is so much more than that, and when you're living your life in the absence of grave stakes, doubt takes on a much different function, one that is useful in virtually every circumstance: as a powerful tool in the maintenance of an equilibrium.

The idea that personal health and well-being is best achieved by maintaining a balance in all things, that is, an equilibrium, isn't new nor should it be surprising. To run at a deficit or excess of anything in particular is generally described as abstinence or addiction, respectively, but even to less extremes, they infer a lack of discipline. Complete abstinence of some things may be wise, playing Russian Roulette for instance, but that doesn't mean that it would be equally wise to abstain from all risk-taking behaviour. Addiction is a feature of human existence, and we all vary in our predisposition to succumb to one addiction or another, but having a few drinks with friends once in a while, or going to the casino when you have disposable income isn't an indication of an excess. Life is nuanced and nuance is life, and a reliable way to determine the trustworthiness of a statement is to detect the amount of nuance in infers; deterministic or rigid perspectives can typically be dispensed with without concern; they stink of death.

The health of a society is often characterized in the same manner, and why shouldn't it? If society is anything, it is the culmination of interests and lessons learned by a group of people, and it is entirely comprised of people and their institutions; it would be peculiar if the maintenance of an equilibrium weren't just as important for society. Overly deterministic and rigid cultural products that are ignorant of human interest and lessons learned should be evaluated on an ongoing basis to determine the extent to which they interfere with human progress.

Laws and policies implemented and enforced by a government should also seek to maintain an equilibrium, or pursue some semblance of one, while simultaneously not infringing on any individual citizen's freedom to pursue their own. Too often do governments, whose existence is justified entirely by their responsibility to the taxpayer whose interests they ought to be upholding at every opportunity, sidestep said responsibility, in the pursuit of their own interests, a private interest, or interests of another nation, and by doing so, subvert the integrity of every citizen and erode democracy. A government representative who fails to uphold the interests of the majority of citizens while still collecting a salary and wielding authority is the worst sort of thief; they enjoy immunity from accusations of tyranny by virtue of being a democratically-elected official, while the hard-earned income of citizens is taken through threat of legal punishment to be spent in a manner other than intended. I am not opposed to taxation, but everyone should demand not only responsible collection, but also spending that coincides with the interests of the contributors. Government spending seems to be done in a contemptuous manner in wealthier nations, that is, in a way that officials have told the citizenry is good for them or the nation, despite it being antithetical to public interests. Western elites no longer seem interested in representing the public, they believe themselves responsible for managing the public, ensuring we don't go astray, because although they believe the public wise enough to have elected them, we're too stupid to know what's good for us. If an elite perceives the public in this manner, they are incapable of pursuing an equilibrium in the public interest due to a requisite feature in managing people being the limitation of human potential through restriction and the mediation of social interaction. Then again, it is said that people get the politicians they deserve, so if we end up with such elites, then the blame could rightfully be directed back at the citizenry. We're all in this together.

Fear and anxiety, mainstays of human existence, are strangely both magnified and mitigated by doubt, although maybe it isn't strange at all, considering an equilibrium pertains to the establishment of a state of moderation and balance. Self-doubt can interfere with all sorts of things, from public speaking to establishing meaningful relationships, and it can get much worse from there, crippling us to the point of pathology. Certainty, on the other hand, while freeing you from such interference, can be equally detrimental, by generating unanticipated outcomes, and potentially catastrophic ones at that. Certainty, after all, is a measure of your emotional commitment to an idea, and not one of objective truth; your certainty could be misplaced, and you may be duly punished when reality informs you of your error.

Certainly Disordered

In the absence of doubt, certainty can transform into something equally as pathological as an anxiety disorder; I refer to them as *certainty disorders*, frequently described as zealotry or ideology. When we are so certain of something to the point that it interferes with our capacity to doubt, we may conduct ourselves in disorderly ways that can cause us harm, either by others less zealous, or by reality itself. Certainty disorders have an additional feature of being able to readily interfere with the lives of others in ways that anxiety disorders do not, and most people with mental illness are more frequently the victims of crimes than the perpetrators of them. People with certainty disorders cause others to suffer and are far more frequently perpetrators of criminal behaviour rather than victims themselves. Even someone who has been victimized, which we've all likely been in one way or another, can quickly take on the role of a perpetrator following the development of a certainty disorder. Mental illness affects more than just the sufferer, but it doesn't generally cause others to suffer as much as the sick; certainty disorders almost always cause others to suffer more than the perpetrator, and sometimes, if the suffering is observable, it can convince the perpetrator of their own righteousness and justify further instantiation in their views and behaviours, which will likely generate more casualties.

Doubt is the bulwark against certainty disorders and the harm that will likely be generated by them to both the perpetrator and their victims. If even a sliver of agnosticism is present in a view, doubt can squeeze its way in, and protect the human mind from worshipping the false idol deeply embedded in their lesser nature. Agnostics are often criticized and labelled as fence sitters, and to an extent this is fair and accurate, but in the absence of certainty, extremism cannot find a proper footing; while there may be nihilistic extremists, there are no agnostics to be found. They may be called inconsequential then, which is only half true and would only be applicable when it comes to a narrow interpretation of the term, but in my experience, very few people are truly agnostic about broad and important issues. Let's say we were to simplify the application of such a term and consider its use relevant in only the most classic and narrow of topics, the belief in God, or a god, or some gods, even then, most people aren't completely agnostic on the topic. It may be that they feel one way or another when it comes to a particular god in a particular faith, but the implications of any hidden hand, one with or without intention, and the substrate within which it is found, are thematically fundamental to human conceptualizations of a higher power, and most people weigh in on them quite readily.

If you remain agnostic about a belief in some variation of higher power, it would not infer that you are without opinion on matters that would naturally extend from such a belief. A belief in a force-less force or some supernatural sapien would generally encourage us to consider the dynamics of our orientation towards it, or if one even exists. What springs forth from such a consideration is clear: virtue, ethics, metaphysics, belief, existentialism, cosmology, and many more concerns that pertain to human life and to what degree we interface with everything around us. Even if you don't want to use presuppositions about this higher power as a basis for inference in reaching conclusions within each of these respective realms, you then become the progenitor of such conclusions and the mechanism by which they are reached. Atheists of all sorts are genuinely concerned with how to navigate these realms absent the influence of a higher power, a testament to the human predisposition to preoccupy ourselves with such concerns, even in the absence of belief. After all, if I don't take my direction from God, then what can I know about the matters for which most people rely upon God? The point here is that the mere fact that a conceptualization of God exists generates concerns in our minds that we feel preoccupied to resolve regardless of whether we believe or not; the idea of God is one well-spring from which human creativity and ingenuity can flow, even if we disperse after only a sip. Simply put, God is the least important thing about God; the characteristics of such a being need not be relevant to what is produced by the human mind as a result of such a conceptualization, and because of this, even if you remain agnostic about the entity, none can afford to remain agnostic about the ethos produced irrespective of belief. This is what was meant in previous writings when I claimed that *doubt is God, and certainty the devil,* because doubt breeds creation and inspiration, and from certainty, destruction and justification are bred.

Doubt is incredibly important in many situations, although many modern proponents of mental health and high self-esteem seem to incessantly promote the need for validation and confidence building. The problem with this is that validating feedback is only sustaining if it's well-deserved and authentic. A falsehood is a falsehood regardless of the intention behind the action, and an illusion will never be able to compete with the real thing. One authentic brick of confidence stacked onto your foundation of well-earned and well-deserved efforts is worth more than one thousand kind words uttered to feed the fragility of your ego. Our individual capacity to doubt the validity of such feedback will assist us in distinguishing between the authentic and the placative. This permits us to recalibrate ourselves towards the truths of reality, and avoid the virtual prisons and falsehoods of an existence shaped by certainty.

Doubt is particularly useful in relationships defined by care, which is something I'll be elaborating upon in the last chapter. When we find ourselves in a position of care for another, doubt challenges our preconceived notions about the validity of our care, and although it may cause us stress, it is an integral part of ensuring that we are conducting ourselves ethically while in a position of responsibility. Alternatively, doubt is useful in determining the legitimacy of care that we receive, when it can assist us in challenging the validity of the comfort we receive within its confines. Challenge is the life force of human existence and when we are burdened with all that life offers, it smooths the rough edges and orients us out of the darkness.

Doubt is the cornerstone of wisdom, and wisdom is the apex of human understanding. Perhaps we can obtain a little of both, together, within the prison of these pages.

B

CAUGHT IN THE TANGLE

———

I *never asked to be born*. A simple statement that is often aimed at a mother's heart or to demand acceptance as an anomaly of humanity, performative and desperate. Regardless of its delivery, it spends little time mincing words; it is declarative and concise whilst directing your attention to something both mysterious and complex. Of course, no one asks to be born; we aren't even provided with an opportunity to make the request, the implications of such a circumstance likely being more cryptic than any mind can cogently conceive.

Beyond merely existing, there is also the case of who is donating their genetic material to create us, by whom we're raised, where exactly, when in time, and at which standard of living; none of these are things we choose either. The list of uncontrollable elements extends from there and stretches out to form a horizon that both beckons and confounds. Our impression is absent from nearly everything we encounter, but strangely, we have a sense that we are nothing more than the amalgamation of such residue, indelibly marked with a history we never knew but are somehow contained by.

Is this what *I* am? The truth is always more complicated than a single question can address, and answers aren't the most reliable things anyhow. I don't seem to decide who or what I am; in fact, I don't seem to decide much, if anything, at all. Furthermore, I am not the genesis of meaning, nor the meaning of the word *meaning*, or any word for that matter. I am either a passenger or a prisoner, and I'm not sure which is worse.

In the Weeds

This existential dread is a feature of human existence, and I am not uniquely a victim nor a recipient, and there is solace to be discovered in the acknowledgement of its ubiquity. We're all thrust into reality on this rock speeding through space in an entirely unintuitive fashion with no clear understanding of what purpose there is to any of it, or if any such purpose could be recognized, or if we'd even be capable of understanding it. The trajectory of our galaxy on a steady collision course with a neighbouring one serves as compelling evidence that the universe doesn't discriminate in our favour, and we may remain undecided about whether it is better to be aware of our future extermination, or to have had our consciousness be rendered incapable of emerging because of our position in a cosmic queue. As a corollary to Tennyson's love, is it true that 'tis better to have existed and died than never to have existed at all? There are compelling cases that can be made for both, and exposure to one with which you may be unfamiliar may stir in you an uncertainty that you'd rather have avoided if you knew what it offered.

A phenomenon that occurs with potentially unknown but certainly unspoken frequency is that of human resentment experienced in response to this dread, powerful and obfuscating for some people in the pursuit of happiness or meaning. Such resentment is mostly rational, but it is gifted wings of feather and wax by the deep well of suffering that we all possess, and it can take flight orienting towards a retaliatory goal. Human experience is one thing, how we manage our responses is another, and how the outcomes manifest in us over a period of time is yet another still. For some, including myself at one time, retaliation is perfectly salient and somewhat exciting due to the path it establishes where previously there was none, and we believe it may lead us out of the abyss. Retaliation conjugates in predictable ways if you understand the human animal, and there are generally four targets: the self, others, a convention, or reality. It is common for more than one of these to be targeted by an individual, but rarely are all four simultaneously on the chopping block. There just isn't enough room, not that I'm trying to limit any of the precocious among us.

Another way of stating all of this much more concisely is: being a human is mostly bullshit.

Crass, perhaps, but it seems to encapsulate the topic relatively well. So then, if this is the case, presuming that no one has had access to the gems concealed in these mysteries, or if there are even any to be mined, what are we to do about, well, *anything*? How are we to define truth? What are the things we may take for granted as being true in order to move forward? How are we to live? Which things may we take for granted as being productive or valuable to assist us in answering this question? What are we exactly? And when we discover things about ourselves that may be true, to what extent do we allow them to dictate or form models of behaviour? Beyond these are an infinite number of significantly important questions that have answers that are typically completely unintuitive and some may remain impossible to answer. Some questions may not even be asking the right thing, or they may be presuming that just because there are locked doors, that they must necessarily each have their own respective keys. I've noticed that it is very common for humans to create keys for doors that don't seem to exist, despite their insistence that every frame contains a throughway.

Before you think that I'll be answering any such questions, I'll tell you that no one book is up to the task, and for some, all of the recorded writings in history offer only a glimpse into what might be going on. What typically occurs is that a field of study is birthed from a single such question, and due to how complex the preliminary evidence presents, dozens of specialties spring forth in order to hopefully have a chance at shedding some light into one of the dark corners of a room that has more walls than any human mind can appreciate with a detailed blueprint.

Entitlements and Prohibitions

My concerns generally tend to emerge from a sense of what I may consider to be true not only from a functional point of view, but also the ethical implications of whatever I land on. The former is not particularly difficult to achieve, as all humans can find at least one thing that functions in our favour more or less, but the latter shares the opacity of most complex phenomenon, especially when we try to wrap it around a human being, with both its known and unknown absurdities. How can I know the material or thread count? How thick or thin should it be? Should the material be rigid or flexible? Breathable or impermeable? Soft or rough? Can everyone be wrapped in the same cover? Is a cover even ethical? Do categories respect the human animal? Regardless, we are certainly capable of being placed into categories not only because they are apparently useful, but also because some are true. What, if anything, can be true for everyone?

This a question I think about with some degree of frequency, and although the specificity of characteristics would likely dictate the length of the list, I believe that even the shortest list has a few uncontroversial offerings. On the contrary, I am highly suspicious of those who believe no such overlaps exist, regardless of whether this perspective is fueled by ignorance or strategy.

What may be extended to me by virtue of my birth? is one such question that has occupied my mind for nearly twenty years. *To what am I entitled? What may I demand and expect to receive?* We all likely have some thoughts, although a consensus is probably rare. A question that I believe is equally, if not more important than these questions, and it is often never examined, is *what may I be denied by virtue of my birth?* There are corollaries to the follow-ups as well: *What may I be prohibited from doing? What may I do and expect to be punished?*

There are compelling observations and ways of legitimately confirming their accuracy in regards to empathy, common knowledge, the universality of human emotions, and a shared evolutionary history that informs a significant amount of our being. This alone should be adequate for most people to believe it is at least possible, if not likely, that there are universal human paradigms, but for the rest, let's overlook these and focus predominantly on a pattern of thought fueled only by rhetoric.

Although I am only ever capable of considering these answers from my own point of view, it is necessary that I acknowledge that anyone may direct these questions inwards, and in doing so, the synchronicity of a dialectic should emerge if we are to cooperate. After all, if I can ask them of myself, then to what knowledge may I privilege myself in the absence of concordant minds and discourse? That is, unless everyone else is a figment of my imagination, or not real in the same way I am, or if I just believe you unworthy of consideration. Barring these exceptions, which I believe to be either untrue or unwise, I would then possess a great deal of responsibility in carefully assessing these answers, for although we are of different minds, is it not simply a matter of puzzling circumstance that my consciousness emerged in me, and yours in you? Could it not have been otherwise? Semantically, perhaps not, but as physical entities existing at one particular place and time, it would certainly seem so. I could've been you, and you could've been me, as least hypothetically for the purposes of an exercise in thought, and this acknowledgement should be sufficient enough to at least have a starting point in the pursuit of both reciprocity and ethics.

Considering the aforementioned questions, there are some words present that carry with them important signifiers and inferences.

What exactly is virtuous about birth? Does being born, despite your lack of consent, impose upon you a high moral standard? And if so, why? And which model is being used to inform us of these standards? Would it be possible to establish a consensus in any of these regards? Is a consensus necessary to produce something of even minor value after such discussions occur?

Are you entitled to anything in life? Can you demand and receive something as compensation for your non-consensual birth? Is it a matter of explicit request, or implied receipt that you receive such things, if any exist? Does this have anything to do with human rights? Is it possible for a natural entitlement to exist, or are they all human constructs? Is there even a difference between these two if we're looking through an evolutionary lens?

Can natural prohibitions be articulated, or are they all human constructs? To what extent should evolutionary principles influence the degrees of freedom in a civilization that may produce prohibition? How much of a consensus is required for prohibition to be established, recognizing that even dissidents will be subject to the rule? What should the scale of prohibitions be? If different prohibitions have been scaled differently, how do we establish the model for this categorization, and what does it look like? Can individuals engage in transience in order to pursue the version of freedom they seek? Should it be easy or difficult, and why?

Punishment

Perhaps the concept with the broadest appeal is the idea of punishment. Humans seem to have a keen interest in punishment; its existence, application, delivery, exemptions, arbitration, longevity, and presuppositions of its efficacy are oft discussed in a rather heated fashion. We are passionate about punishment, and while some of the reasons why are elusive, there are many philosophical and psychological insights that penetrate deeply and reveal why we find it so compelling not only in discourse, but as a matter of private examination. The reasons vary greatly of course, and there is likely to be some variation in their configuration in each of our minds; I dare not speculate about the grotesque imagery present in the minds of those obsessed, not because of fear nor disgust, rather it is due to my own familiarity with such imagery, and a desire to respectfully preserve those you've concealed.

A persistent and mystifying feature of punishment, however, is the human failure in accurately predicting when it may surface, and what may be found in its wake. Often, it is unclear what form punishment takes; can we always tell when we are being punished? Can punishment and justice be the same? Some people seem to believe they are synonymous; what may be said about this framing, or those who believe it, if anything? How often are we the perpetrator of a thought or action and also the one dispensing the punishment upon the offender? Are we not far more often guilty of ill-advised thoughts and actions than how frequently we encounter punishment, even if it's justified in correcting our shortcomings for our own benefit? And thank goodness for that! It means we don't need to be perfect, and it demands that we uphold and engage in regular applications of forgiveness not only for the sake of one another, but for our own sanity. Be wary of those who seem incapable of forgiveness, they aren't likely to be good company.

Entitlements, prohibitions, and punishments all seem to have some relevance to virtue, because in its absence, how are we to determine if we've transgressed? Seems straightforward enough, but it becomes immensely complicated when we pursue, at any scale, how to define virtue, whether it be ambiguous or unequivocal.

There is often far more conviction about which metrics are suitable than anyone has any business standing upon, and far more models available to rely on any single one in the pursuit of stability and meaning, despite the overconfidence that many faithful espouse. There never seems to be a deficit of certainty in the singularly-minded, and the palpable ignorance of their trailblazing failures stokes in me equal parts laughter and discomfort.

The Virtue of the Vicious

Tell me again, what is it that you were certain was going to change the world?

Wait, let me rephrase that, because it may unfairly criticize a view as being wholly whimsical.

Tell me again, what is it that you were certain was necessary to do to change the world, despite the fact that it may seem, or be, unsavoury?

Yes, that's much better. These things need to be done, and you aren't doing it because you want to, you feel a legitimate sense of duty in carrying it out. You're a soldier in the war of restoration of the true definition of virtue. Not *your* definition, *the* definition.

At least that's what people tell themselves, and what people who think alike will tell one another, all the while unaware of the fact that, despite our understanding of physics, they've all managed to miraculously occupy a place in both the circle, shoulder to shoulder, and on their knees in the centre, mouths opened and ready to catch. The singularly-minded are magicians, and their specialty is self-deception, and for the ambitious among them, there aren't enough eggs in the world that can be broken to make their omelette, despite the glee with which they dutifully destroy henhouses.

Tangled Gravity

Despite any predilections we may have about a mind that both gives and receives itself, this sort of feedback loop is probably most fairly characterized as *human*. Common features of human thought reliably produce such feedback, but humans aren't constrained by such feedback, not entirely anyhow. We can have all sorts of foreign influence enter our proximity, shifting and warping the orbits of our thoughts and perceptions, and by extension, our behaviour. Some of us welcome even the largest meteors to crash into things with reckless abandon, and some will insulate the integrity of their solar system with so many bulwarks, even space dust won't find its way in. Regardless of our tendencies at any given time, or for how long we maintain any pattern in particular, they need to be substantiated in some way in order to justify their existence, even if only to ourselves. Not all require the same amount of justification either, as this varies greatly depending on the circumstance, the product, and the mind.

In the pursuit of discovery, we rely on various models to assist us along the way, whether it be for convenience, placation, utility, or truth. Some of these are religion, philosophy, secular humanism, natural or common law, social justice, evolution, cosmology, mathematics, intuition, and there are many more to be sure. These are all adopted with the intention of gleaning some amount of insight that may guide us in how to live, or at least how we *should* live, regardless of whether or not we follow it. Embedded in the dictates of any of these has to be an ethos, an appeal to the character of the subscriber, that although it may not be suitable for everyone, it is at least a worthwhile pursuit for them. The amount of dedication to any of these generally says more about the subscriber than the model itself. The desire for proliferation is determined by their enthusiasm, and demands for enforcement are measured by their ego and their comfort with an authoritarian worldview.

We aren't shackled to any one of these in particular, a truth implied by an evolutionary history and realized throughout our lives. Some people are more beholden to one or more of these models than others, and differences in our personality lend either advantages or disadvantages in breaking free, but it can be done to be sure. Never underestimate the power that ideas possess to liberate a human mind, or their potential to tether us in place, destined for a life of bondage.

The Freedom of the Frame

These ideas that can liberate or tether, how can we differentiate between them? Is there some reliable way to distinguish them from one another? Maybe a feature? A framing? The demands they make of you? What they promise? How they make you feel? How they instruct interaction? There is valuable information to be gleaned from such answers, and many will be covered in this book.

What about disagreements between the value of those that liberate and those that tether? Is it always the case that more liberty is preferable? Perhaps, but disciplined and measured conduct that may be difficult to obtain in the absence of limitations may interfere with unlocking hidden potential that could only emerge through a balance of the two. This isn't controversial to state, but what if we took it further? Is there value to be found in a life of bondage? Do we enjoy being completely tethered, freed from the pain of uncertainty and unpredictability? Does the cage beckon in our hearts? My immediate reaction to questions of this sort is to respond in the negative. After significant contemplation, my response upgrades to a confident dispensation of arguments that purport that a human life is best articulated through servitude, regardless of how literal or artistic the perspective. To live is not merely to exist, and anyone that would reduce a human life, even unintentionally through purely intellectual conceptualizations, to that of procreation and labour, is no friend of mine. Be cautious of those who would recommend a way of life that places you in some variation of existence that is antithetical to that of a living animal; they are either ignorant of their own nature, of history, or they are very well informed, and rather they are seeking to subvert your humanity and reduce you to a cog in a machine.

While caught in the tangle, how can we ascertain truth, or a mechanism to guide us towards something meaningful? What does truth look like? How can we identify it? There are a few ways, but some are more reliable than others, and even then, some truths aren't as valuable as others. Focusing on specifics alone isn't generally useful, and although logic science provides us with a great deal of assistance in parsing cogency in this realm, cogent arguments do not infer truth by default. This is why arguments or approaches that rely on a single or small-sized sample of evidence aren't often convincing to a skeptic, nor should they be. We all have stories of things we've heard or seen, or people we know that exemplify something or another, yet these are fundamentally insufficient in constructing even a simple argument that would pass a basic logic test. Logical fallacies exist precisely to assist us with figuring out whether or not things make sense in the hopes that, if we sufficiently avoid them, we may be pursuing truth, and even then, there's no guarantees; we don't know what we don't know.

I'm not the first person to describe truth as a *pattern*, and it's possible you've encountered this in other places. The reason that describing truth as a pattern is attractive is because phenomena that tend to be true over time infer that they possess some resiliency and reliable variance in their application, which makes them easy to generalize. Because they take time to recognize, we need to keep our eyes peeled and our ears opened and take in as much information and experience as possible so that a pattern may emerge in the weave of existence. If you don't pay attention, you may miss truths that surround you from every vantage point, and hunt you like prey.

Γ

THE WOVEN TRUTH

───────

I previously recorded a podcast episode that examined the question *How many legs does a dog have if you call the tail a leg?* It was an examination of the different models of thought you could adopt in answering questions in order to produce a functional answer, and then I compared the answers in order to assess quality and truth. The purpose of this episode was to offer insight into human thought so that I could recommend a specific model that would be the most likely to produce coherent outcomes that are concordant with reality, and by extension, potentially truth. My conclusion was that the model of thought that produced the answer *four* was more correct than any other model, and that if you wanted to be the most successful in life, find the most reliable meaning, and have the best chance of long-term stable mental health, it would be wise to adopt the same model. This was simply a thought exercise, but despite my clear framing, I received correspondence from a listener that contained an admission of her disdain for terms like "four-legged friend" when referring to many animals, as her experience working in a veterinary hospital exposed her to a litany of admissions that resulted in the treatment of animals with a missing limb. This wasn't at all the focus of her correspondence, but it stuck out to me as I read through her thoughts, and it is a point worthy of discussion, especially if you've never been exposed to a conversation on the truth or accuracy of categories.

My reply to her addressed most of her questions or thoughts, at least insofar as I could in a few paragraphs, and I wrote a decent amount with regard to her criticism of my conclusion that dogs indeed have four legs. What I briefly touched on, and what is particularly prescient in what I intend on furthering in this book, is how truth isn't well characterized by way of rigid specificity, it is best thought of as a pattern, woven into the substrate of human perception. This is why claiming dogs have four legs is true, but that claiming that not all dogs have four legs is also true. They are both true, one by pattern, and the other by circumstance, but their contextual applicability varies incredibly. If we adopt a model of thought that informs our perception by way of pattern, and the answer that is produced is four, then we are likely to be right more often than not, even in the vast majority of individually observable circumstances. On the other hand, if we adopt a model of thought that informs our perception by way of observable circumstance, and the answer that is produced is something other than four, then we are likely to be wrong more often than not, as it suffers by a failure of applicability to other circumstances, as well as a failure to sufficiently demonstrate a pattern that would constitute truth. Patterns are a superior model to classify truth over circumstance, and the combination of the two is the birth of nuance. They have a hierarchical relationship, but they are not in opposition to one another; the shortcomings of individual circumstances inform the wisdom of pattern, and the failure of universal applicability of pattern informs the wisdom of the specificity observed in circumstance. Besides the perceivably immortal nature of death and taxes, is there any better way to define truth than this? Nuance is the wisdom produced by knowledge of both pattern and circumstance, filtering the totality of information to which we are exposed; truth is embedded in this framework, to be mined by time and effort.

Story Arcs and Types

The complex nature of truth is rich and mysterious, like the humanity that tracks it. As a result, we try to find ways to capture its essence in a useful way so it can be transmitted to other minds. One of the oldest and most reliable ways we do this is through the creation and distribution of stories, which are among the most prolific ways to maximize memetic spread. To assist us in more specifically characterizing truth, we try and find patterns embedded in stories, and these can be characters, plots, settings, introductions, climaxes, conclusions, atmosphere, literary devices, and a host of other useful elements. The coalescence of a particular set of elements that form a recognizable pattern is frequently referred to as an archetype. Although this wouldn't be the traditional application of the concept, to tie up the loose end, the fact that our canine friends have four legs is a dog archetype, but that doesn't mean every dog has four legs. It means that, generally speaking, dogs *should* have four legs. This isn't an ethical judgment of dogs, not that they'd be in a position to take offence anyhow, it is a formal description of dogs based on the human perception informed by pattern that is true regardless of the existence of deviations that are also true.

Even if archetypes aren't true in a literal sense, they are at least meta-true, that is, they are true in a way that, despite literal conjugation, they certainly appear to be valid and applicable to human existence in reliably predictable ways. Archetypal themes act as a sort of proxy for the scientific method in storytelling: we observe an element, make a prediction, perform the experiment of making our way through the story, and see if our hypothesis accurately predicted the outcome. The question here is: what is informing our hypothesis? Why do we seem capable of recognizing story elements in a way that permits us to make predictions that seem to make sense, even in the absence of experience? Even young children listening to a story or watching a movie take offence when the story doesn't go as expected; how do they know what is expected? Why is it that some stories have an ending that makes sense and affirms the psyche—or doesn't, and offends? These aren't mysteries. Despite any belief in texts being handed down to humanity by deities, stories spring forth from the minds of humanity. Stories are reflections of ourselves, and the best stories that survive the ages do so precisely because they are riddled with archetypal themes that resonate with our existence.

Archetypes are truth embedded in the literal and fantasy elements of stories, waiting to be mined by time and effort. They are reflections of our humanity that may be woven into stories, intentionally or not, and encrypted in a way so that others can see their truth, regardless of whether or not we possess the capacity to crack them. Regardless of culture or era, stories are human constants and they are ubiquitous to humanity without exception. I believe there to be a noteworthy correlation with human neurobiological narrative formation based on memories, and I would wager that story creation and archetypes are a feature of our existence informed by our biology that imprints stories in the same way our brain imprints data. I am not in a position to do this digression justice at this time, but it is certainly interesting.

Jung and Old Themes

Carl Jung is particularly well-known for his efforts in trying to give shape to human archetypes, and he produced a significant body of complex and compelling writing fleshing out these archetypes so that we can hope to glean truths about ourselves. You don't need to be familiar with his writings in order to follow where I'll be going, but it is a worthwhile journey if you have both the time and the nerve to be confronted with elements of yourself that you may have previously thought were a secret or a riddle. There is only one archetype that I intend on expounding upon, a sinful one, and one that I see everywhere in the modern era in ever-increasing numbers and potency, to the apparently completely unaware purveyors of said ethos. It is also my sin; it is the devouring mother.

For the uninitiated, when I refer to the devouring mother archetype, I am not necessarily referring to mothers, or even women. In fact, I'll be referring to more than just people with it. Mothers and women certainly possess the capacity to have this feature of their existence direct their conduct in meaningful ways, but so do fathers and men, and I see it manifest in groups, organizations, and governments as well. The thing about archetypes is that they are a human truth, and not particularized to one sex or state of existence. It is true that Jung and others typified certain archetypes as being male or female, but this was believed to be the case as a matter of recognition for their tendency to be more prominent in one sex or the other on average, both in literature and real life. Prominence in one sex on average doesn't mean that it can't be prominent in the other sex, and a lack of prominence of any archetype doesn't infer its absence in anyone. Archetypes are like masks that any of us can wear, and although it seems clear that men prefer some masks and women others, we each have an old dusty bin with the complete collection at the ready. Jung described the traditionally female masks that men wear as the Anima series, and the traditionally male masks that women wear as the Animus series. Well, he didn't describe them quite like that, but I didn't want to quit my mask collection analogy, because it's sweet.

So then, if an archetype is a symbolic representation of truth informed by pattern, and certain archetypes have been recognized and appreciated as offering legitimate insight into humanity, then what is the devouring mother archetype? How is it characterized? What is an example? Important questions, and all of them will be answered. Briefly, however, I believe it important to give the devil its due, and offer some context to assist us in appreciating why certain archetypes exist, and why, despite the obvious pitfalls that some infer, do we as humans permit them to guide us towards an immoral and disastrous end? The short answer is *meaning*; but let's examine this a bit more in fairness to any would-be sinners among us.

Mothers of Meaning

Humans are preoccupied with meaning, and if you aren't, it is likely you've either never done anything meaningful, and as a result, you've never experienced the high it provides, or you've yet to live a sufficient enough time to have learned that the pursuit of meaning is among the most reliable treatments in easing any existential dread that may plague you. Furthermore, a reliable mechanism to obtain meaning, which has thankfully become far more explicitly discussed in modern times due to people like Jordan Peterson, is the accumulation of responsibility, that is, the voluntary acceptance of a burden that challenges your capacity to bear the weight. This has been known for a long time, but it is yet another grain of historical wisdom that has become lost on the shores of our presumptuous modernity. It may seem antithetical to some that taking on a burden would provide you with meaning obtained through competence, with an orientation towards becoming powerful that conjugates into freedom, but it often turns out this way. Essentially, burdening yourself creates freedom, at least from the constraints you impose upon yourself in the pursuit of happiness. It is counterintuitive, but true nonetheless, a testament to the human reality that meaning can never be offered or given, it is earned through effort and accomplishment. Placation and comfort are low resolution stand-ins for meaning, and you will hunger for nourishment despite being full.

The devouring mother, whether literally or figuratively, occupies a position relative to that of someone in their care; they are responsible for them, whether this be deliberately or simply as a matter of circumstance. It can be perfectly legitimate based on common social dynamics, such as a parent and child, or elected representative and citizen, or it can be an assumed position absent legitimate social context, such as a stalker and their victim, or an activist and their special interest or specific disenfranchised group. One is an obvious dynamic that appears to have a compulsory component based in reason and reciprocity, and the other is one where the dynamic materializes in the mind of the initiator and the dynamic is absent consent or coherence. Regardless of how like you'd like to characterize either dynamic, there is meaning to be found in the adoption of a burden, and even those of unsound mind or intent experience the allure of this calling. Humans crave meaning, and we aren't always aware or concerned about what may be produced, intentionally or otherwise, as we are caught in the gravity of our sense of purpose.

The devouring mother feels compelled to act as a guardian, driven by duty, who both protects and placates. Unfortunately, this orientation is parasitic, as any mother or guardian must be, because in the absence of their burden, they are categorically destroyed. A mother without child is no mother, and a guardian without a charge guards nothing but a hope for a vulnerable party to present itself, and when it does, the guardian becomes whole. I'm not attempting to be insensitive to mothers who have lost their children, I am making a statement of categorical meaning, and not one of human predisposition. A mother may indeed guard the memories, the belongings, or the gravesite of their child, but they are no longer a mother burdened by a child, their grief has become their burden, and over time this won't provide meaning, only sorrow. It is no less a human reality than any other, but a mother cannot devour grief and remain sustained, they require a life force from which to draw meaning.

It is for this reason, I hope, that we can recognize that what drives a devouring mother is no less a valid human quality than any other, but the sin persists. Recognition of this personification does not infer condonation, acceptance, nor respect, at least not beyond the respect we may reserve for another purely by virtue of their humanity. It is generally immoral to sacrifice the life force of one for that of another, despite dynamic or covenant, however it does complicate things when someone voluntarily sacrifices their life force for another, but relations with a devouring mother do not typically concern these outliers.

THE SONG AND THE SWALLOW

The devouring mother consumes, but it would be worthwhile to clarify what she consumes. To re-iterate, the devouring mother occupies a position relative to someone in their care, and through this relationship, they receive meaning. Because humans crave meaning, this is something they enjoy, and for some, they enjoy it so much that nothing else quite compares; the sense of purpose it provides nourishes the human soul like nothing else. What the mother will do over time is begin to interfere with, or diminish the capacity of their child in their development, consuming their competence, potential, and emotional stability, rendering their child incapable of comfort or survival outside of the kingdom over which she reigns. This establishes longevity in the dynamic that defines both parties, one as the protector, and the other, the protected; their existence is co-dependent, and if the devouring mother succeeds, she will drain meaning from those in her care until she meets her end.

Manifest Mothers

Predicated by a desire or a need to be needed, devouring mothers may sabotage the growth of those in their care to establish a reliable source of meaning in their lives, a bottomless well from which to drink. Governments that survive off of tax revenue have a similar vested interest in diminishing the capacity of the citizenry to reach their potential, establishing a reliable target to support through programs and services, justifying expenditure that would otherwise fall under significant scrutiny. As long as the public needs, the government can provide, and they will always establish new programs and initiatives to broaden their grasp and accumulate more power and influence. There is much to be gained by keeping the citizenry incompetent, and it also makes them less capable of competing politically to wrestle the reigns away from their "representatives." The devouring mother may even instill a sense of guilt in her children at the thought of leaving her, providing additional support in maintaining the relationship. A government does much the same, using emotional weaponry on a large scale to coerce the sympathies of the public and discourage opposition, at least in open discourse. *"How can you be against this initiative that helps the disenfranchised?"* they will ask, and the glares that accompany the leading question with loaded language will typically be sufficient to silence you and recognize who is in control. Silent consent is sufficient for this sort of government, you don't need to agree or like it, just keep your mouth shut and keep paying your taxes. Keep in mind that initiatives don't need to actually be effective at correcting what they set out to address. The priority is public relations and accusing the public of insensitivity should they disagree with any proposal, instilling a sense of guilt in them for demanding a reasonable explanation, and perpetuating the parasitic relationship. *Do what Mommy says and everything will be fine; the Milgram experiments weren't real.*

Despite an obvious axe to grind due to the deterioration of accountability and efficacy of my own government, it is natural for these dynamics to surface in the hearts and minds of conscientious individuals that possess a genuine care for others. Their care and concern have become pathological, however, and they'll intend good things for everyone as we all descend into the depths of hell. In a sense, sins are pathological iterations of virtues, so while some care and concern are welcome, a complete absence is callous, and an excess suffocates; the maintenance of an equilibrium emerges in all things.

While I've commented briefly on some manifestations of the devouring mother archetype, there is one in particular that will serve as the foundation of this book, one with a salient composition and relevance to humanity with which few stories can compete. Medusa is well-recognized as a manifestation of this archetype, although I've found that much of the dissections don't do it justice, and leave behind an emaciated corpse in their wake. Much of the mythological malpractice that I've encountered is being done by way of special interests that seem to be obsessed with characterizing Medusa as a symbol of terrifying femininity that should either be feared, celebrated, or both. This is one way that the story of Medusa can be interpreted, that is, if we consider it prudent to purchase a choice steak and feed it to a dog. If Medusa is an archetype, even if it is the devouring mother, then her value as truth informed by pattern is squandered if we limit the applicability of her symbolic power to only one sex. It reminds me of arguments over whether God is a man or a woman; a tone-deaf exchange that mischaracterizes an entity that is traditionally uniquely positioned to serve as a powerful force so that some may find solace in whether God has a penis or a vagina. If the feature of Medusa or God that is most worth examining is their sex or which sex should be more concerned with them, then I fear people may be missing out on the potential value that can be extracted at the conclusion of an appropriately thorough and earnest journey. I intend on making my contribution in this book.

That being said, a song must first be heard before we encounter the swallow.

Δ

THE SONG

⎯⎯⎯

T here is a common yet strange human experience of being drawn towards something, salient and obscure, a sensation of warmth that beckons us, calling our name and suggestive of fateful consequences. Despite a lack of any specific understanding as to its genesis or why we may be susceptible to it, it is an invitation to do more than simply exist, it is an opportunity to live, and not just any sort of life, but one that promises fulfillment through meaning. The outcomes of this pact, should we partake, cannot be guaranteed, but we often decide that nothing meaningful can be gained if no risks are taken, and we are swept off on a journey, ignorant of who, or what, may be our bedfellow in this bond. Often the goal towards which we become oriented is unexpected, magnifying the mysterious nature of things that we encounter through epiphany, and some of which can be so unexpected that they persist as deviant, and remain unspoken, forever unheard by even our own ears.

A more general question could be posed: *why do we wants calls?* Or perhaps it is more appropriate to consider that once we've heard a call, *why do we seem inclined to follow them?* It may be an invitation to live a life comprised of more than just the status quo, but there is something else happening as well. We perceive these songs as valuable on a fundamental level, much deeper beneath the surface of the call to adventure. The tug of a song is visceral, we can feel it in our bones, puppeteering us as if our life depended on it. Many of us feel like we *need* orientation, however this doesn't mean that we spend any time thinking about *why* we feel this way.

Throughout human history, there are countless examples of people improving themselves and their surroundings, seemingly just for the sake of excellence, or being the best, regardless of what it is. The simplest and most straight-forward motivation is to improve our prospects with regards to mate selection, and this is likely to be virtually ubiquitous for most contexts. The more status we accumulate, the more eyes will take notice, and if these eyes perceive value in us, they're more likely to dedicate themselves to us, even if it's only for a night. Whether additional benefits exist beyond mate selection or are intertwined with it, they seem to exist nevertheless; the complexity of human consciousness prevents us from having it so easy.

There has to be a sense of incremental improvement or progress in our life, despite how minor the incline may be. Although it may seem obvious, the concepts of improvement and progress infer orientation, otherwise towards what exactly are you progressing? Improving on the shadow you've left behind only makes sense within a conceptual framework where it can be measured according to some standard, and it is the relationship between your shadow and your goal that give your measurement coherence and relevance.

We feel *good* to be part of an endeavour that is successful, particularly when we've dedicated a significant portion of our lives to it. A single small step forward is encouraging, but it isn't significant enough to produce a sense of purpose. Orienting ourselves towards something provides us with a roadmap, but meaning is only ever obtained at the conclusion of the journey. It is the high we experience from achievement that informs us that meaning flows forth from orientation, and in these moments, we feel powerful in the face of our accomplishments.

When we start to make changes to our diet in the pursuit of better health, for example, these confirm our capacity for change and they are encouraging. While these are a good start, and we may have improved in some sense compared to our shadow, this is precisely the point when people give up or fail. Small improvements are necessary to reach a desired goal, but if meaning is what you're after, the small boosts that these palliative moves offer will run dry before long. It is only when you've made the complete transformation in implementing your diet permanently and you're actually healthier that you can look back at your shadow from a great distance and be satisfied with a sense of fulfillment that can authentically nourish your soul. This is why we should seek out difficult things in life, and ravage the feast of their conquer.

When your bank account is empty and you've decided to save for a house, accumulating one thousand dollars after one month is a start, but it's not enough for a house. This is because saving for a house takes an incredibly long time, and if the housing market continues on the same course in Canada, most young people will never be able to afford one. I'm not intending on mocking anyone, but the reality is that saving a small amount can be done by most people, that doesn't make it an achievement, but when you've saved enough for something special that you really want, especially when it took a long time to earn, then you will feel capable, in control, powerful. Progress is important, but the sorts of achievements that provide meaning through orientation aren't easily accessible without the burden of responsibility. Making it to the third step in recovery is worthy of recognition, but completing the twelfth is an achievement that can lighten the burden of existence.

When I decided to write a book, getting a framework was useful, and completing the first chapter was nice, but as any writer may tell you, this is nowhere near a book being complete, and many outlines and chapters collect dust despite our best intentions. I had a full-time career, a part-time job that demanded a good amount of my time and energy, and a burgeoning relationship that I was trying to invest in while I was writing this book, and when I had moments of free time, writing was the last thing I wanted to do. I was tired of working all the time, tired of the pandemic, tired of seeing my fellow citizens turn on one another over straw-man arguments and a desperate desire to return back to normal life; I was just tired in general. That being said, I spent more than a year trying to squeeze in writing whenever I could, acknowledging that if I kept myself oriented towards my goal of producing something meaningful, eventually I'd make it to the end. My hope was that I would make something that may encourage others to self-reflect or pursue wisdom, or at least maybe to think more dynamically, and that was worth it enough for me to continue writing. It was only when I had completed my first manuscript that I felt any sense of relief. When the first manuscript was done, I was still nowhere near being finished the book, because in many ways, I was just getting started, but I still felt like I had done *something*, and this book isn't even that long.

The point I'm making is that in one sense, the risk of dedicating yourself to pursuing a call is worth it, but in addition to this, the meaning that flows forth from the orientation towards something that requires dedication and the burden of responsibility is one of the best ways to justify your existence to *yourself*. There is a concern, however, one of such significance that it may compromise the entire endeavour: how can we distinguish between orientations? Are some good and others bad? Are we effective at recognizing when the pursuit of our own excellence crosses the line from ambition into psychopathy? Ambition has a tendency to instrumentalize others, and in some cases, this can have mutual benefits, but when we become unconcerned with how we are instrumentalizing people, or the effects this has on them or others, we have crossed a line into deviance.

I have experienced one such deviant call, and rather than keep you in suspense about its nature or depravity, I'll say it plainly: *I planned on becoming a vigilante, with all of the potential activities that accompany such a pursuit, and was motivated by what I assume are reasons similar to anyone who adopts personal risk for the perceived benefit of others.*

You probably weren't ready for that, so I'll let you read it again, and then I will elaborate a bit to confirm that you are not in fact hallucinating, nor are you confused by what I may have meant.

I planned on becoming a vigilante, with all of the potential activities that accompany such a pursuit, and motivated by what I assume are reasons similar to anyone who adopts personal risk for the perceived benefit of others.

Like many people, I believed that many things could be better than they are, and that the reason for the unacceptable state of things was due to a combination of deliberately oppressive actions by the powerful and the laziness or indifference of the weak. Everyone was to blame, but it is more righteous to defeat the powerful and protect the weak, and in doing so, balance will be restored to the universe. Or something like that anyhow; specificity is often lacking in articulated justifications of power, either due to the incoherency of the conjuror or a mindful attempt to conceal thinly veiled despotism.

While I will elaborate on the details that contributed to the development of such a desire and what I had planned to do, as some features are common and relatable, and others darkly humorous, it isn't the focus of this chapter, nor of this book. It will, however, serve as a backdrop for a resonant archetypal theme that I am going to expound upon: the orientation of humanity towards that which beckons it.

What exactly is this emergent and enigmatic call from the ether? I don't know, and pretending to know is for the foolish and cynically ambitious. No one really knows, but there are some good attempts at trying to clarify the phenomenon. Although I enjoy the occasional dive down a rabbit hole, my interest for now is to elucidate on the human experience of such a call, and examine the dynamics of its draw. A good starting point, I feel, is an examination of what may constitute the progenitor, at least for human comprehension, and I'd like to illustrate this phenomenon with the sirens of Greek mythology.

What is a siren exactly? Even the stories themselves have inconsistencies, but let's start with a functional model.

A Siren is an Alarm

Whether they're depicted as humans, birds, fish, or some combination thereof, they generally represent deception, and a deadly one at that. They produce a song, heard by either the ears or the minds of hapless sailors, that lures them towards a rocky coast and ultimately to their demise, their vessel shipwrecked and the sailors drowned or stranded until starvation. A siren is a creature that sings, and their song does only one thing: it captivates the listener with promises of glory and truth, provided they stay the course and seek out the source of the beauty. Whether the captive is greeted by a beast or a beautiful woman is irrelevant, sirens do not offer kindness nor consolation, they merely sing, and their treachery is only ever recognized when it's too late to change course.

In a sense, they represent the concept of fate, or perhaps the threat of fate, whether it be perceived as literal or conjecture. The word siren is an iteration of the Ancient Greek word *seirá*, which denotes a cord or rope, because through their song you are bound, or entangled, on a journey with a predetermined end. Follow the dulcet tones of a song that promises a predetermined end at your peril, for there is no living in a life bound by such an end other than death, and no meaning to be found on a journey that materializes out of thin air. Unless, that is, you desire a life that liberates you from the pain of choice while convincing you that you're in control? Not that I'm in a position to make judgments about such things, but we can learn a lot about ourselves by considering why we may be susceptible to some songs and not others.

We seem to crave the freedom to choose, but we enjoy the relief of a decision made by another; it's curious, isn't it? This is an oversimplification, of course, as our measure of satisfaction is typically dictated by how closely the outcomes of decisions made by another coincide with our desires, and in those cases, it is often more than relief that is experienced; it feels like justice, like something has gone right with the world. How frequent it is that we perceive justice precisely at the moment that our ego has been fed. Perhaps the siren's call reaches us before we even depart, and we are propelled forward to set sail on treacherous waters, allegedly of our own free will, so that we can experience the sweet release of captivity, just so that we may be relieved of our will to live. Such an existence is horrifying for some, and a pleasant dream for others. I suppose it all depends on how much value you believe yourself capable of producing in the absence of servitude.

There is a perfectly cogent evolutionary explanation pertaining to resource management that would sufficiently explain the positive emotions we experience when a favourable outcome is produced without having to contribute anything ourselves, and a concise elaboration could likely be articulated. I find such explanations valuable in the pursuit of truth and they offer me a sense of inclusion in a ubiquitous existence predicated on a shared biological history that offsets the divisiveness of unhelpful and oversimplified categorizations of complex beings, but my unease persists nonetheless. This isn't a criticism of evolution, rather it is an obvious acknowledgement, at least to me, that organisms with a sense of self and complex emotions require more than a single framework to be satisfied with what may offer insight into our human condition. Evolution carries more than its share of the load of human existential explanations, and the insights that it offers are far-reaching and tempered, probably much more so than most people are aware, but it doesn't seem to be able to carry the entire burden, whether this is due to a legitimate limitation or one birthed from the poverty of human emotional stability.

Despite what you profess, believe, or know, there will always be gaps in our understanding of *something*, and this is one thing that makes us susceptible to such calls, so that we can focus on something that we believe worthy of pursuit; this orients us towards a goal, and we often feel drawn by this orientation, animated by a sense of purpose. This is something humans need, and if you need it not and your understanding is gapless, then you have become a victim of ideological possession, and such a spirit will bend you to its will and silence all other songs that may be heard.

The siren's call is sweet and consoling, but its product is rigid and predetermined. Ideology can be recognized by the deafening silence it produces; when truths become conclusions, and we are less than the recipient of an outcome decided by another, we are subordinate to an idea. This is a different sort of servitude than one where we relinquish our capacity to choose in the face of existential dread, where our relief is our own to the benefit of ourselves, despite the questionable long-term outcomes it produces. Ideological servitude is an external force that demands you relinquish your capacity to choose not for the relief we experience in doing so, but rather for the benefit of an idea, and the outcomes are never for your benefit because it was only ever promised, it was never seriously a consideration. Ideology offers relief because it eradicates your humanity and replaces it with a will of its own, and it confuses our sense of orientation with one of destiny. It is due to these characteristics that although rigidity of thought may offer relief, it isn't the sort you should want; it is antithetical to human potential.

Inspire and Amuse

The siren song is an appeal that is hard to resist but that, if heeded, will lead you to an undesirable conclusion. The idea elicits in me an image of a beautiful woman whose beauty alone sufficiently triggers me sexually, but upon her first utterance, she is reduced to an empty-headed pretty thing. Such is the difference between a siren and a muse. A siren captivates, a muse inspires.

In one story, Hera, the queen of the gods, persuaded the sirens to enter a singing contest with the Muses. The Muses were Greek goddesses who ruled over the arts and sciences and offered inspiration in these realms. They were the daughters of Zeus, the king of the gods, and Mnemosyne, a Titan and the personification of memory. It's interesting that the Greeks believed that it made sense to connect memory with royalty and inspiration in their mythos, as if to infer that there is wisdom to be found in a relationship between knowledge and power, or perhaps, that knowledge is power.

Most stories that survive the ages do so precisely because they remind us of lessons that time may permit us to forget, and some are more memorable than others specifically because the lesson they teach is of such significance, that it would be a sin to forget them entirely. Without knowing the details of such a story, what is your prediction for the conclusion? Keep in mind that truly resonant stories seem to intuitively make sense, although we often lack the capacity to articulate exactly why. How would a siren fare in a competition with a muse?

There has to be an appreciation for what is attributed to historically relevant fictional characters and their respective stories, because it is in these attributions that we find the breadcrumbs leading us to human universality, or at least what we believe to be. When the attributes of a character or the themes of a story are unintuitive or appear to be at odds with our perceived expectations, it offends our sensibilities and some doubts often manifest as to the value of the work. Whether the plot or conclusion are horrifying or conciliatory is typically of no consequence, they just need to be justified, or make sense, whatever this means.

You may have guessed that despite the ancient Greeks having a proclivity for antagonistic success in their stories, the Muses handily defeated the sirens in a contest of song. This seems right, doesn't it? Like justice? Perhaps just like the sort of justice we perceive when our egos have been fed? There is something about the swift dismantling of a representation of treachery that we find so satisfying, it brings a smile to our faces. It's a powerful gust of wind that pushes the mist away from our path, and we are consoled by the clarity ahead. Of course, the Muses won! A siren always loses to a muse! Let's dive into the rocky coastline and examine why this seems to makes sense.

An appropriate place to begin with such an examination would be the beginning, wouldn't it? What is the respective genesis of the Muses and the sirens according to their tales? Origin stories are of particular relevance for characters because they frame their future trajectory in a manner relative to foreseeable catalytic circumstances. Origins do not necessitate outcomes, but they offer insight into how we are to interpret the character's archetype. I've provided a few simplified character origins, framings, and outcomes in Figure 1. It is important to remember that characters are distillations of human truth, so while we may see ourselves in them, they are only a part of us, and our complex nature and reality will not conjugate well into these outcomes despite our best efforts. They are characters, we are human.

The Muses are the daughters of Zeus and a Titan, which is among the most prestigious and noble beginnings, if such a thing exists, and in their own right, carry with them all of the status and

STORY	CHARACTER	ORIGIN	TRAITS	FRAMING	OUTCOME
Star Wars	Anakin Skywalker	A slave shrouded in mystery	Great potential, prophesied to restore balance to the Force	Fueled by fear, desires power to save wife who died while birthing	Consumed by fear and desire for power; met demise at the hands of his own son
"Joker (2019 Film)"	Arthur Fleck	Failed clown and comedian, dark past, lives in a city rife with violence and poverty	Neurological issues, adopted, poor, malnourished, regularly mocked	Cannot access meds, past becomes clear, ridiculed by his hero	Anti-hero, villain, murderer
Game of Thrones	"Jon Snow (Aegon Targaryen)"	Bastard of respected noble, secret identity	Brave, foolish, honourable, lost between two worlds	Outcast, survives death, caught in political turmoil, identity is revealed	Holds numerous presitigous positions before finally becoming free
"The Little Mermaid (1837 fairy tale)"	Ariel	Mermaid princess, burgeoning womanhood	Naïve, curious, impatient, foolish, selfish	Falls in love with a human, bargains with a witch, foolishly risks her own life	Dissolves into foam, given chance to earn a soul by doing good deeds for 300 years
Harry Potter	Harry Potter	Orphan of unknown origin	Scarred, dormant powers, meek	Discovers parents murdered, uncovers dark plots, target of assassinations	Becomes increasingly powerful, endures hardship but ultimately defeats evil
Breaking Bad	Walter White Sr.	Chemist, high school teacher, drug kingpin	Terminal lung cancer, family to support, resentful of former colleagues	Manufactures crystal meth allegedly to support family and pay for treatment	Begins enjoying crime, generates conflict, attempt resolutions, dies from a ricochet bullet
Carrie	"Carrietta N. White (Carrie)"	High school outcast	Shy, lonely, telekinetic powers, unstable mother who beats and imprisons her often	Endlessly bullied by peers, attends prom under false pretenses, doused in pig's blood on stage	Uses powers to kill mother and others, peer reveals she also has powers as Carrie dies in parking lot
The Lord of the Rings	Frodo Baggins	Orphan, hobbit of the Shire	Diminutive, apprehensive yet courageous, honourable	Thrust into a catastrophic conflict, voluntarily bears a great burden to unify the races, ventures into nearly certain death	Succeeds in destroying evil due to the support of a close friend, internal conflict persists

Figure 1 - Destiny of story characters based on their origins and traits, framed by their respective story and catalyzed to produce a particular outcome that resonates with us as human beings.

power that accompanies being a goddess. Now, just because you're a goddess doesn't mean you can't be dethroned and have your existence reduced to squalor; the Greeks weren't without their sense of irony. On the other hand, Greek mythology is riddled with examples of gods behaving badly yet never facing the comeuppance that we all feel they deserve, a testament to the reality that powerful evil forces exist in many forms, even within us, and they need to be accepted for what they are, despite the injustice with which we label them. Life is, after all, structured in a manner beyond our control, and it takes all sorts to make the world go 'round, regardless of whether or not you like or condone it.

The Muses inspired, whether by choice or by design, and through their influence feats were made possible that could never have occurred in their absence. The word inspire has a particular connotation, and it is universally applied to the Muses instead of one of many other words that could convey something similar. To be inspired is to ignite a spark in us so that we can produce something that is a reflection of our own heart or mind's desire; it is not the same as being captivated. It is also not the same as being influenced or convinced, directed or inclined, manipulated or forced, all of which imply that what we may produce isn't entirely what we desire, it has been pushed, in a manner of speaking, by a hand other than our own, and it serves at the pleasure of another. So then, for the Muses, being born of the gods and occupying a position serving at the pleasure of others so that we may be inspired to produce for ourselves causes us to justifiably perceive them as righteous, kindling embers within us so that we may breathe fire. How does this compare to the sirens?

The origin of the sirens is less fleshed out than that of the Muses, but there is enough recorded to play with. They were believed to be fathered by the river god, Achelous, and mothered by one of the Muses, although there are conflicting accounts regarding which. They were companions of Persephone, who was famously abducted by Hades, the god of the underworld. For their failure in intervening in her abduction, Demeter, Persephone's mother and goddess of the harvest and fertility of the earth, gave them wings to search for her, and when they still failed to intervene, they were transformed into sirens and banished to an island near Scylla and Charybdis. It is here where they must remain, singing at every opportunity to captivate sailors and bring them to their demise, and should their song ever fail to capture a human soul, they shall immediately perish; their existence is now defined by deceit.

The sirens captivate, and bind us to a fate where the only outcomes are their survival and our demise; they do not ignite anything in us, they suffocate our potential and extinguish our lives. They do this while being bound themselves, to an island and to a singular purpose; they project their fate onto us so that they may continue their life of servitude, with no concern for the lives that they entangle, it is now their purpose. The sirens served at their own pleasure, and failed twice to protect the most important thing to Demeter, her daughter, who was taken by the god who reigns over all souls, and as such, now continue to serve only themselves, and only for survival, so that they may shepherd souls to the underworld, where Persephone now resides with Hades. So then, the sirens, born of the gods but occupying a position in the periphery of value, but not of value itself, disobeyed the gods and failed to prevent the abduction of Persephone, and Demeter, who made their lives most comfortable up until their transformation, served only themselves, and continue to do so at the expense of mortal souls. It is for these reasons that we perceive them as self-righteous, and justifiably destructive and deceitful.

If we are to extract value from a thematic point of view of the Muses winning the contest, it is that the righteous defeat the self-righteous, or that they should at least be perceived as more valuable, or more worthy of celebration. There is a simpler way to interpret this story though, one bearing clear connective tissues with reality both in contests and beyond, and it concerns the importance of authenticity in human existence. The reason that a muse will always beat a siren is because they are an authentic representation doing battle with an inauthentic representation. The song of a muse inspires you, and it provides you with a spark so that you may be permitted to serve at your pleasure, and if you follow the sound to the muse, you'll be met by a beautiful entity, godly and interested in your humanity. The song of a siren captivates you, and with it your freedom and your ability to serve at your pleasure, and if you follow the sound to the siren, you'll be met by a twisted monster, ungodly and indifferent to your humanity. The real thing will always beat the counterfeit, and although both of their songs are resonant, authenticity liberates, and falsity confines.

A possible Abrahamic description of this phenomenon would be that truth is found in an orientation towards God, and that deceit is found in an orientation towards the devil. Not that its bestowal would necessarily be done by either, but rather it is the course and catalogue of our orientation that determines whether our nature becomes transcendent or regressive. There are many analogues for this sort of dichotomy in most religions, and it remains pervasive in stories due to its archetypal tethering. It is for this reason that although I consider myself an atheist, God and the devil certainly exist; religious belief isn't necessary for a religious idea to be true, despite its lack of corporeal tangibility.

Song Susceptibility

Parsing such songs often isn't easy, and they often present equally pleasing and valid, but like most things, the devil is in the details, and if you don't read the fine print, you may become an accessory in your unbecoming. It is also worth mentioning that many things can affect our song susceptibility, as well as how likely we are to discern between who may be singing. I've yet to meet someone who doesn't believe themselves to possess good judgment, despite the number of eye rolls and stifled laughs present when they profess how discerning they are; then again, we are far more apt to lie to ourselves than to others, psychopaths excluded. Whether we possess good judgment or not, it doesn't mean we exercise it, and regardless of how frequently we do, it will always be limited by a number of things, both internal and external.

Internal and external limitations, or perhaps more broadly, modifiers or influences on human judgment, each have their respective areas of examination, the former through psychological frameworks, and the latter informed by socio-cultural phenomenon. These can't be fairly assessed in their entirety here, but it's worthwhile addressing some of them briefly to help frame the concept of song susceptibility.

I have been fairly characterized by people as being more interested in the internal workings of people than external forces, and I tend to place individualism higher than tribalism in the hierarchy of human ethos. The reason for this is because as an autonomous person, which we all are, our internal workings are more accessible to us, and we have a greater degree of control over the extent to which we permit or deny features of ourselves to flourish when compared to external forces, even if this control is limited. It's not that we cannot assist in our own way in shaping externalities, but they are far less accessible and sometimes impossible to alter, especially if they are rooted in reality, which will swiftly assert itself and inform us of our foolishness. I can best control and dictate myself and my thoughts, at least insofar as I can, and as such, I prioritize internal workings as the worthiest of understanding and consideration in the face of a world over which I do not reign and cannot accurately predict with much frequency.

Some common internalities that limit the exercise of good judgment are anxiety and depressive disorders, which will prioritize relief and avoidance above the long-term benefits that good decisions produce when exercising good judgment. Disorders that alter perception will often prevent our capacity to make reasonable judgments about anything, however this is predominantly during an episode. Fear can significantly limit our capacity to do the right thing, our cowardice trumping any courage we may be able to summon. An underdeveloped pre-frontal lobe, which assists in orchestrating the litany of our cognitive heuristics, impairs our ability to exercise good judgment, as we see in teenagers (and we experienced ourselves) who have yet to fully grow their brain. Difficult situations and dilemmas challenge our capacity to exercise good judgment, and we will often choose the path of least resistance. Incentives can significantly compromise our judgment, especially if we are presented with a short-term solution that will allow us to procrastinate and deal with the reality at a later date. The recognition of our own talents or shortcomings may either propel us forward or cause us to withdraw in lieu of determining the best course for long-term benefit or stability. Conversely, little time spent introspecting will render us ignorant of our own tendencies and produce results in decision-making that don't serve our interests. Desperation drives us to do insane things sometimes, and guilt can often drive us to the same extreme.

There is also the matter of being lost, or perhaps, bound to nothing in particular, which makes us particularly susceptible to the siren's song, because otherwise we will wander aimlessly, and we may be inclined to follow anything that offers solace. The unbound seek a cord by which to become bound, it seems, which, despite how much weight you give to external forces, appears to be a human universal.

The list goes on and on, but they all have something in common, which is that we all have the opportunity to grapple with any of these if we choose to do so. The outcome is uncertain, but the mere fact that these are ostensibly accessible by our own minds places them in a category of phenomena that should, at least in some part, be receptive to our feedback.

The Trap of Externalities

External forces certainly exist, and they are no less important in characterizing social animals than internal workings; both have influence on the intrinsic elements that configure humanity. That being said, I've noticed that those who prioritize socio-cultural phenomenon as the best lens through which to define, examine, and explain humanity frequently transgress in two ways: one is a matter of strategic intellectualism, and the other, a failure of empathy. Please allow me to explain.

The intellectual sin is one of ignorance of the nature of the organism being examined, whether it be deliberate or laziness. In order to pre-suppose the validity of a socio-cultural explanation being prime, you would need to be completely disinterested in the inherent features of the thing upon which the external forces are acting. A lack of appreciation for the composition of that which is susceptible to influence, whether it is innate or purely a product of feedback from previous influence, is to waste your time; if a human has a nature, or obtains a state of existence predicated on external forces that shape it, it still has an identity of some sort, that is, an internal working that can refer to itself as *I*, and it would then be incumbent upon you to become expert in what comprises the self-referential entity so that we can make predictions about how future influence may act upon it.

If you mix a clear liquid and a white powder together, the results are entirely unknown unless you've correctly identified both the liquid and the powder, and there are thousands of each. If the liquid is water and the powder is sugar, then you'll get sugary water. If you heat it and reduce it, you get simple syrup. If we have vinegar and sugar, the result is salad dressing, and vinegar and baking soda make an eruption for a papier-mâché volcano, and we can mix water and flour to build that. Water and powdered magnesium react and produce hydrogen, and low-oxygen water will cause white phosphorous to produce a toxic compound. Strong acids mixed with cocaine produce pink and blue waste material, and the same acids mixed with powdered peroxides will ignite and melt through various materials. It doesn't matter which is the internal or the external substance in these reactions, what matters is that if you introduce something to another, despite how benign you believe them to be upon first glance, the nature of the materials matters because they dictate the outcome. We can make compelling and accurate predictions about human biology, behaviour, and cognition, and as such, it infers that there are things that we *know* about ourselves, despite any romanticism that may compel us to presume a blank slate. Pleading ignorance isn't a compelling defense for irresponsible chemistry.

Even if you believe that humans are entirely socially constructed, you still need to have a healthy understanding of the perpetually fluxing pattern that we represent over time in order to make coherent statements about external forces and exactly how they shaped such an entity. This is rarely ever done. My suspicion is that avoiding the scientific products of biology, psychology, and evolution is done either because such avoidance benefits the aims of the social constructivist, or because it's harder and more rigourous of an endeavour than perpetuating purely intellectual and baseless philosophies that lack constraints by design; like I said, deliberately ignorant, or intellectually lazy.

The failure of empathy that lies in the heart of the socially-obsessed may seem like an unfair accusation, as frequently it is these same people that espouse the most concern for others, especially the downtrodden, however this is defined. This is also done particularly loudly with simplistic slogans, which apparently constitute relevant argument and righteousness and not the petulance and fragility that we tend to observe. One of the biggest issues with the framing of the socially-obsessed is that externalities are often characterized not as an explanation for human conduct, but as an excuse, which reduces humanity to a simple object that merely heeds a call because it is present, like a zombie reacting to a thrown stone. This would mean that all of us, except for the socially-obsessed observer, are merely pawns, yet *they* have somehow broken free from The Matrix, and they possess not only some sort of awareness that eludes the rest of us, but they're also benevolently trying to wake the rest of us who still sleep. This is not only a failure of empathy, but it's also a triumph of the ego. They are awake enough to choose for themselves and reap the fruits of their labour, the rest of us still sleep or are otherwise incapable of seeing what they see; they are the shepherd and we are the sheep. How is it we've come to applaud these people?

Some external forces that can shape us are social pressures, real or imagined, that we feel should be respected in order to make our way in the world. There are specific social contexts that may demand adherence in one way or another, and failure to acquiesce could produce some minor discomfort or a violation of the self, or something much more serious depending on the stakes of the situation. Our proclivity for group allegiance will direct our judgment towards making decisions for the sake of the group, regardless of whether or not it is good for us or anyone else. These can be so potent as to dictate our outcomes for us as our judgment has been replaced by an orthodoxy that must be upheld at all costs and in every situation, or else it may crumble, or so purveyors would claim. Ignoring any obvious value that any orthodoxy possesses for now, which is traditionally implied and taken for granted, we can feel the effects of numerous externalities simultaneously, each jockeying for position in the hierarchy of your decision-making. Family, religion, and political allegiance have a tendency to dictate the limits of our judgment, restricting some avenues while making others permissive, even when we would otherwise consider them low quality or unreasonable. The extent of their influence will be determined, however, by how much stake you place in each, and how they fare when weighed against other internal and external forces.

Something you may notice is that for every external force, there is some measure of internal input or feedback that is necessary as a feature of the negotiation of existence. It isn't a matter of which is more important or powerful, although I obviously have my opinion, but regardless of how you prioritize them, there will always be some aspect of our behaviour that is informed or shaped by our conscious engagement. We all experience internal and external pressures, no one is immune to their effects, but there is variance among us in which things we succumb to. Simply because externalities can invoke a tendency doesn't eradicate our capacity to deny its call. You're more than a puppet, and socially-obsessed thinkers would seek to reduce you to one so that they can attach the strings they deem worthy and make you dance to a siren's song.

Assuming our accuracy in characterizing the righteousness and goodness of our pursuit, many roads will present themselves to us, each varying in length and treachery. If you only see one road, then you're hearing a siren's song. When many roads are available, we need to parse the goals from their mechanisms, because we may still be bound by a siren, destined to meet our demise and take others down with us. To what extent can we identify whether or not our chosen path matches the intentions that propel our goal forward? Do you know how to tell the difference? Does your ego permit you? With honesty and careful examination, we might be able to do this. Let's examine some situations where it isn't always obvious that we're on the right track.

E

TRAVERSING THE TUG

———

Regardless of which call is heard or which direction our orientation tugs, there is the matter of identifying our position in the schema. It could be simply a matter of ego that places us either in the centre or the periphery, but despite any differences among us, calls tend to draw us in and tease out a sense that they are designed for us alone. It affords us the privilege of not only being the protagonist, but also the conductor, as if to be simultaneously God and incarnate; a bifurcated entity that both orchestrates and leads. Upon receiving a deviant call, what sort of mind places themselves in a position to dictate that lives must be taken, and that they are tasked with carrying it out? Despite any qualifying expertise that may exist beyond personal experience, I believe I can shed some light on the subject; there is, however, a distinction I'd like to make first.

There is a difference between a goal and the mechanism we employ to reach it, and even when we are of sound mind, we aren't particularly good at predicting what certain measures will produce. This is generally why it is always good to have a specific goal in mind, and then implement specific measures that will best serve as the mechanism to achieve the desired end; no plans can produce guaranteed results when humanity is involved, but it gives the best odds. This is why virtuous conceptual goals like progress, equality, equity, peace, and unity don't tend to produce results that will be universally recognized or appreciated, because we all have different perceptions of their depictions in reality, provided that you would support any of them in the first place. I don't believe myself cynical when I describe these words as being meaningless in a practical sense. If, however, there is a specific goal in mind that is predominantly influenced by a desire to achieve something like progress, and it is articulatable, coherent, and practical, then it is far more likely that it will be realized in a manner that will be identifiable by those who take notice. Do not give your allegiance away to anyone bearing an ambiguous banner of progress; the devil lurks in the ambiguity of polite language.

I had a goal in mind, one just as benevolent as any modern progressive axiom, and the road was equally paved with good intentions, just as the destination was veiled as utopia, a mirage disguising the hellscape of a yet undefined reality. Mechanisms can vary greatly, and most do not include the physical harm of others, but when your goal is a better world, you start to believe any means as worthwhile, and sometimes, necessary. The amount of stake you place in your mechanism may be magnified by the extent to which you believe it to be novel or original, or that it simply hasn't been done on the scale you're intending, and this can feed your zealotry. You'll do what no one else was willing to do, either because they lacked the insight or the stomach, regardless, you're special, right?

I've noticed that there is often significant discordance between the goal and what the mechanism is likely to produce. Apparently, the axiom *violence begets violence* has been forgotten, and our ability to predict obvious outcomes that certain mechanisms will produce seem to be absent social discourse, likely due to either cowardice, conscienceless partisanship, or a perverse monetary incentive. It is only in the mind of the confused that sowing chaos will generate sustainable order, unless order or peace was never really the goal in the first place. Peace can certainly be the stated goal, but how are we to respect or follow someone that implements plans where the mechanism is at such great odds with the desired outcome? They're either a fool or a liar, and neither deserve your trust or allegiance.

There is also the consideration that the goal is being concealed as the mechanism. This veiling has been plausibly speculated in explaining the genocides in both the USSR and in China, where the death tolls were so high that they've become difficult to accurately estimate. What I'm describing here is that these regimes were either ideologically possessed to the point of insanity, or that the goal was the mass-murder of its own citizens, and not one of the necessary mechanisms that occurs as a by-product of the blazing trail towards utopia, as was claimed. Sometimes it is just about killing and torturing. It makes sense to describe it in this manner as sometimes violence manifests at the hands of the desperate or possessed, but it also manifests at the hands of the violent. Violence begets violence, and the violent also beget violence. Pathologically violent people that desire power over others can be a protester, a neighbourhood stalker, or the aggressor in a relationship, but they can also be the leader of a movement or the head of a state. In fact, it isn't even particularly difficult to navigate a system with well-established standardized processes and workplace cultures with clear incentive schemes. Even a moderately intelligent person can hold a position of influence in a government if they adopt a game-theoretical approach and take the time to learn the rules of engagement. Any ambitious malcontent that adopts the right approach can manoeuvre their way into power. The western world in particular is a paradise for the sociopathic, and I'm not sure why this isn't discussed more regularly in an attempt to keep people apprised of when a wolf may be hidden among them.

The Reflecting God

The similarities between this and religious extremism should be apparent, but there is a significant and noteworthy distinction that can inform us on how to best engage with someone who believes themselves on a crusade, and it concerns who sits atop the throne. There could be a lengthy psychoanalytical digression on the marriage of religious belief and the ego in justifying action taken in the name of a higher power, but the blurred lines of the psyche aren't what I'd like to focus on while making this brief point. Ultimately, ideas have incredible power, and if someone believes themselves in the service of a higher power, especially one that is articulated in a religious text, then they are arguably orienting themselves towards God, who sits upon the throne at which they kneel. In the absence of something like a deity towards which we orient ourselves, we are likely to be in pursuit of an ethos birthed from something wholly distinct from any entity in particular: a rational framework. These may both be pursued with equal ferocity, but some do not glimpse God on the throne when they kneel, they see themselves, or someone just like them. A school shooter and a suicide bomber do not worship in the same way, but they have a lot in common, and we can observe similarities in their sense of obligation and their duty to act; they are cleansing kin. A discussion about mental health could rightfully be had right now, as the pathologically violent and religiously obsessed have both been depicted as suffering mentally in their own right, but that doesn't nullify the comparison.

It is my belief that in most situations, regardless of scale, people that produce poor quality or disastrous outcomes did not have evil in mind as part of their goal. That being said, we are often sufficiently incompetent at identifying evil clearly, especially when it's present in our mind. I'm not evil, right? I'm doing something for the benefit of another, or for my child, or for society; how can I be evil? Correct, most people aren't evil, but that doesn't mean we won't produce evil inadvertently, and the unchecked character flaws that may sow such chaos are typically fear, ego, or ignorance. You could be really talented and be fearful, egotistical, and ignorant not only about the flaws of your mechanism, but also the flaws themselves, and then you're really twisted, and people will suffer by your hand. Machiavelli should have become a parody of poor-quality thinking in modern times; it seems rather that some view his rhetoric as aspirational. I blame educators.

There are some reliable mechanisms to reach certain goals, and some goals that people will reliably orient themselves towards. I offered assistance in navigating this territory by encouraging you to answer the calls of a muse, and avoid those of a siren, as well as how to distinguish between the two, but more can be done in characterizing why such deviant calls exist. Song susceptibility isn't purely a matter of internal and external pressures, we are susceptible as humans by definition, as a feature of our existence. Providing guidance in this regard is available in large quantities through self-help books, and although I believe I am trying to help others with this book, I wouldn't call this a self-help book. There is an inherent problem with helping others when we discuss orientations and meaning, which is that we run the risk of either misleading others with an inappropriate goal, or we may inadvertently poison the well. I have deliberately tried to avoid providing any specific goals, as I believe there are plenty of minds being filled with ludicrous aspirations in the modern era by parents, teachers, activists, and politicians, and I do not wish to be included among them. I wish for you to orient yourself, and I encourage you to ignore any guidance that rings hollow or generates discord; I am just trying to place warning signs. A main focus of this book will be to examine one warning sign in particular, a character from an ancient story that is still appreciated and recognized for her potency more than two-thousand years after she was initially conceived. Her name is *Medusa*, a gorgon and manifestation of the devouring mother.

F

THE SWALLOW

———

It is possible that you've been waiting patiently for an elaboration on my previously mentioned vigilantism, with all of the questions we typically put forward during an investigation. Personally, I'm partial in most situations to *why*, but in my experience, people seem disproportionately interested in *who, what, when, where*, and *how?* While these other questions can certainly provide tasty morsels, *why* is the only one that could ever hope to sufficiently constitute a meal. It is possible that many prefer these for the same reasons that we enjoy thrifty and saturated messaging, entertainment, and food, because they are all easy to access and they trigger our emotions more readily than their alternatives. Gossiping may be more fun, but you don't really get at the heart of anything when it is consumed, and it is done deliberately for personal excitement with no consideration of an authentic or high-resolution understanding of the subject matter; it is heartless and brainless. This doesn't mean it doesn't have value, it's just that we should limit how much junk food we consume, whether it be literal or an analogue. For your interest, I will share all of the details, at least the ones that I recall with some amount of clarity while being mentally sick, before characterizing it in a manner that you may find sustaining.

I planned on becoming a vigilante, with all of the potential activities that accompany such a pursuit, and motivated by what I assume are reasons similar to anyone who adopts personal risk for the perceived benefit of others.

Who I planned on targeting isn't particularly interesting, as I believe is typically the case when violence is a consideration. It's always someone that the aggressor believes is a worthwhile target for some reason or another in lieu of a more creative alternative that requires more work and is likely less destructive. Violence and destruction are often a lazy shortcut for both aggressor and aggrieved alike, the latter feeling particularly justified as they perceive their violence to be retaliatory, righteous, or retributive. My worthwhile targets were criminals, in particular ones that seem to elude the hands of justice, always just beyond the reach of a system limited either by principle or corruption, the distinction being of no consequence to a mind on a mission. It is essentially like trying to be a literal crime fighter, and although I've never liked comics or heroes, I certainly understand the interest and the allure. All things are permissive when you're answering a righteous call in the pursuit of adventure and a self-issued license for justice, the same frame of mind adopted by terrorists and tyrants. The reasons fictional heroes get a pass from public scrutiny are twofold: their in-story conduct doesn't directly affect reality in a way that we would need to manage their outcomes, and, due to their archetypal nature, we can see ourselves in them, and them in us, in a manner that is obvious that they are dramatically simple representations of humanity. We are much more, after all, than whatever can be encapsulated by a single fictional character, and so we shouldn't expect that they sufficiently represent the totality of humanity nor realistic concerns that we are required to grapple with on a regular basis. Vigilantism, terrorism, and tyranny are parodies of the human condition, perverted to the point of pathology, and awakened by a siren's call. There are no prisons suitable for some people, right? Even if there were, they'll find a way to elude a sentence or settle on parole, right? They'll continue to harm their community and generate conflict where peace would otherwise reign, right? Punishment is the only mechanism to prevent the innocent from being victimized, right? If only it were that simple.

The *what* has been established already; the harm and potential death of whomever I've defined as destructive forces. I'm still uneasy writing that sentence and reading it over, a reliable feature of truth being that it tends to challenge comfort. Let's move on.

When these would occur is less precise, as I lacked a concrete plan, and it would depend on whether you believe the act itself to be the sole event in question, or if it was when I took my first step down the road to destruction. I first began struggling with my mental health for a variety of reasons in October 2003, I was twenty-one years old and enrolled in university. My mental health continued to deteriorate over time and in early 2004 I had decided on my fate. I began taking karate and eventually joined the Canadian military as a reservist under the impression that they would offer me discipline and skill sets that may be useful to me on my new path. I broke up with my long-time girlfriend that I loved deeply and had every intention of marrying, a gesture that I justified as an act of dignified kindness, to protect her from any trouble I may attract in my new life. I look back at this decision with great remorse, and I recall with impressive detail how callous and aloof I was when I ended it with her over the phone; her tears and confusion haunt me to this day. It is incredible how jarring a sense of purpose can be in bringing out the worst in you.

The factors that guided me to this point aren't the subject of this book, but I have elaborated somewhat on them in one of my podcast episodes. The reason that such violence was avoided is due in large part to a meeting I had with a close friend of mine in the late summer of 2004. I quit university and ended my relationship, while I had begun to develop an ever-stronger sense that I was approaching the precipice of meaning. I arranged to meet a friend of mine at a local Tim Horton's coffee shop in Brampton, fully confident that his reception to my plan would be nothing less than enthusiastic and supportive; the delusions of a desperate soul, I suppose. I had decided that I would need help, and I was looking for a partner to assist me, after all, the bond that can be built and strengthened between two friends risking their lives for the good of the downtrodden would be extraordinary, right? The desire to feel such a bond weighed on me heavily, despite the fact that I had just severed one with my girlfriend; the sense of the sick is never sufficient enough to purchase comfort. It was only after I had shared my plan with my friend that it became clear to me that I might have a problem. You see, I wasn't met with conscientious praise, I was met with concern, not with words, but with silence. The power that an expression possesses can be so potent as to save lives, it appears. It was the deafening silence, the absence of a call, that washed over me, leaving cracks in my certainty and permitting doubt to seep into my psyche. After that day, I became consumed with doubt, lost inside myself, perpetually just barely beyond the warmth of a flicker or a flame. I didn't learn to be still; I became still.

I want to make it clear that I was willing to follow through with my plans, I wasn't discouraged due to a lack of nerves or ability, nor of any clarity of thought. Rather, my progress was stunted by an opposing force, one of concern, of care, that liberated me from the confines of my own prison. The opposition created doubt in me, and doubt challenges the bondage of certainty, and the destruction of certainty liberates. This is the moral imperative embedded in the exchange between two minds that disagree: the realization that you could be wrong.

The events that follow are documented in the same podcast episode, and I never followed through with any of my plans. I received help and despite any progress I made, I was incapable of reconciling my relationship or my education, predominantly due to my shortcomings in managing such difficult and complex human circumstances. It is what it is, I suppose, a testament that nothing is ever gained chasing a siren's call, and there will always be casualties of the heart and the mind, and sometimes, human lives.

Where was wherever my path may have taken me. I figured that a lion fears no part of the jungle, and I was foolish enough to believe that humans could be analogized as lions; only psychopaths believe themselves lions. The truth is that they are parasites, who may only flourish by consuming the life force of hosts, and in their absence, they wither and die. This does not a lion make.

How it would've played out isn't too dissimilar to anyone else who imagines themselves to be on a path in the pursuit of an ideal future, I imagine. I would be flawless in my execution, masterful in my planning, outsmarting everyone at every turn, applauded for my efforts by the appreciative, and envied by the cowardly. Precise, powerful, cunning, and righteous. Humans have powerful imaginations. I've yet to meet anyone with even half the amount of competence or righteousness that they believe themselves to possess while grappling with grandiosity. It is part of why Live Action Role-Playing exists, and why modern egotists like Antifa and Neo-Nazis have been cynically yet correctly described as LARPing. To be clear though, it is only the ones wearing medieval garb and wielding swords that are aware they're playing out a fantasy and nothing more, the latter are just assholes, mislead and lost, but assholes nonetheless.

The *why* began to establish itself within the first pages of this book. It is my belief that there is nothing particularly unique about me, at least not in this regard. Orientation, doubt, belief, struggle, mental health, archetypes, humanity, and reason are universally resonant in ways with which few other things can compete. They are features of humanity, present in everyone and visible to anyone that pays attention, and their ubiquity is part of why I focus on them so much; I tend to be anti-special interest.

I will say this though: I understand why people pursue paths similar to the one I abandoned, and they are often noble, at least in the mind of the believer. This is what makes improper orientations based on a simplistic understanding of the world so dangerous. It is typically done in the pursuit of care for others, to be a guardian, or to protect a community. It is also about having a sense of control over something, generally because we feel like we have no control in our own life. I wanted to do it because I wanted a sense of purpose, to be loved by others, to feel like I mattered. While these may be reasonable and perfectly understandable to many, doing the right thing isn't sufficient, it must also be done in the right way, and I was wrong. We all have images in our mind of our desired outcomes emerging necessarily after we carry out our burden, but how are we so certain? Have we fallen victim to the wrong song?

Song susceptibility is a feature of our humanity, and although not everyone succumbs to a limiting and binding tune, the potential for any of us to be tethered persists, given the right circumstances and reinforcements. The human condition is a perpetual state of existence that employs us all, and our tenure only ends when we breathe our last breath. There will be clear differences in how these manifests in each of us, and distinct songs that guide us astray, the totality upon which I cannot comment nor describe. Archetypes are particularly useful in this regard, because even if your *why* isn't the same as mine, we may have more in common than you realize. Let us shine a light on the sin and sinner, to illuminate Medusa, and give definition to the devouring shadow she casts.

Of Maidens and Men

Archetypes occupy a peculiar space in human existence. They are conceptual products birthed by human minds, but they inform us of truths that may remain a mystery in the absence of their presence in stories; they are conjugations in the feedback loop of our perception. They don't often convert very well in a literal sense, and sometimes they don't at all. To my knowledge, there have never been any humanoid hybrids donning a head of writhing snakes whose gaze can turn any living thing to stone, but that doesn't really matter, this isn't how archetypes work, and attempts at literal translations sufficiently fail to produce anything more than cheap fanfare. Archetypes are fragments of our complexity, potent in presentation, and they can generate consequences that are orders of magnitude more prescient than anything in our lives. We can permit them to possess us in the real world, but don't expect any elegant storybook conclusions.

There are variations of the story of Medusa, and you may prefer one over others, but for the purposes of this book, I will be combining all of the elements of which I am aware to form the most complete version of her story, with enough details to sufficiently explain all the relevant components of the archetype. Stories and myths are consumed by us as if they occurred according to some legitimate corporeal chronology, and this is why sometimes we perceive inconsistencies as to exactly where and when these things happened, as if this makes sense. Some stories, or perhaps just some versions or details that are added later, do not consider the earthly realm and its spacetime framework when such changes and additions are made. This is why some elements seem foreign or out of place according to what we expect as recipients of stories, and we may even debate about what the real or true details are of one or another. This is to be expected, and what I believe is occurring when some details persist and others dissipate with time is that the resolution of the substrate sharpens over time, and what remains are versions that we find most valuable, whether it be by wisdom, by popularity, or both. What is wise isn't always popular, and what is popular is almost never wise, but these do overlap from time to time, and I believe that the story of Medusa is among one of the better examples, should it be explored deeply enough, in mining an adequately rich pantheon of human truths.

The most complete version may be considered uncouth to the more proper among us, but thus is life, a warzone harbouring natural disasters. The main character in this story is a maiden named Medusa, who is cast in her role as the herald for humanity. I'll provide an overview of the finer details, and then an elaboration will follow.

Medusa was a servant of Athena, the goddess of wisdom, to whom she devoted her life. This devotion was not only comprised of a willingness to care for her temple and honour Athena, but also a duty to remain celibate, and place no other desires above her worship. Medusa caught the eye of Poseidon, who had a particular affinity for her golden blonde locks. Poseidon seduced her, and when Athena discovered their affair, she punished Medusa by turning her hair into writhing snakes, and cursed her so that if she ever met eyes with another living thing, it would be turned to stone.

Medusa, twisted by the wrath of Athena, fled from the temple and her home, trying to find sanctuary. She continued her journey, further and further away from the warmth of familiarity, and ultimately ended up on the island of Sarpedon, commonly referred to as the end of the earth. Sarpedon was entirely populated by the blind, who could not see her for what she had become, but were also immune to her petrifying gaze. This is where she resided, away from anything living, in a cave with statues of wandering wildlife who were unfortunate enough to become bystander decorations of her lair.

Perseus, the son of Zeus, who has his own sordid tale of deceit and revenge, was manipulated by Polydectes to kill Medusa and return with her head. Polydectes did this because he wanted to marry Perseus' mother, Danae, which he believed would be impossible while Perseus still lived, his overly protective and interfering nature well-known to Polydectes. This would result in certain death for nearly anyone who dared to confront Medusa, but unbeknownst to Perseus, the gods had already decided that he was destined to kill Acrisius, the king of Argos, and he couldn't very well do this if he were dead. As a result, the gods took a keen interest in his quest to kill Medusa, and he received many gifts to aid him.

Among the gifts was a shield, polished to a mirror-finish, that he received from Athena. This was given to him so that he could approach Medusa without looking at her directly. He travelled to the island of Sarpedon, approached Medusa while she slept, and beheaded her, retaining her head in a special pouch for the return journey. From the severed neck of Medusa sprang forth Pegasus, a winged-horse, and Chrysaor, a man wielding a golden sword, brothers birthed by her death, and fathered by Poseidon.

Poseidon was angered not only due to the death of Medusa, but also because Queen Cassiopeia, mother of Andromeda, boasted endlessly about the beauty of her daughter, who she claimed was even more beautiful than the nereid, sea nymphs, daughters of Poseidon and known for their beauty. Andromeda was also destined to marry Perseus, who had just returned from his journey to the island of Sarpedon. Poseidon sent the Cetus, a giant sea monster that he kept caged deep in the profound of the sea, to attack the kingdom of Cassiopeia, to serve as a reminder that the gods cannot be challenged.

Fearful of the attack, Cassiopeia chained her daughter Andromeda to a rock at the precipice of the kingdom, in hopes that her death alone would appease Poseidon and spare her kingdom. Perseus confronted the Cetus, retrieved the head of Medusa from his pouch, and directed her gaze at the Cetus, turning it to stone, the power of the gorgon still present. The Cetus broke apart and sank into the sea. Perseus freed Andromeda from her chains, and prevented the attack on the kingdom. Perseus and Andromeda were married, and the fragments of the Cetus were placed in the stars as a reminder not only of Perseus' bravery, but also as a warning against anger and jealousy, in particular, the sort on display by the gods.

Despite my previous clarification, I want to remind you that this story has numerous archetypes embedded within, some are known to be traditionally male, and some female, but the fact that one character is a man or another is a woman is largely irrelevant. Certain characters may resonate more with you than others, but any of us could find ourselves in the position of Perseus or Medusa given the right circumstances. It's even possible that we condone the actions of Athena or Poseidon, behaving in a manner that is both godly and jealous. Stories have characters, themes, plots, beginnings, and ends, and all of these can be archetypal in nature; it is up to us to recognize which of these resonate with us at any given time, and take heed of which lessons may be learned. It would be foolish to deny yourself potential wisdom that may be gleaned from stories due to some discordance based on sex or position, which is why the concepts of the anima and animus are integral to archetypal understanding.

Although I am one to dive directly into cold water on a hot summer day, let's dip our toes just below the surface and slowly immerse ourselves, taking time to acclimate to the temperature before introducing another inch into the cold and cloudy depths below.

The Devil's Due

The English name Medusa comes from the Greek word *medousa*, which literally translates into *jellyfish*, but also means *guardian*. It is the feminine present participle of the word *medein*, which means to "protect, or rule over." When stories are conceived, decisions are made on every element, some quick and some slow, and part of this process is considering which elements should possess embedded meaning. It could be coincidence that these words inferring care and the tendril-like hair of Medusa resembling the tentacles of a jellyfish happen to line up perfectly with compelling symbolism and recognized archetypes, but it is unlikely to be the case. Of the millions of stories ever told, there has to be at least a few that contain elements that conspicuously tether to human reality and meaning, and it could be simply a matter of chance that the one I've selected is a sampling error, but as we submerge further, it will become clear that this likely isn't the case. Coincidences are a feature of life, that is, at least insofar as they may be articulated observations by us when we perceive a connection, regardless of whether they are genuine. If we adopt an evidence-based model in this instance, however, at some point we will have crossed a threshold and entered a realm where we've witnessed a sufficient number of coincidences that a pattern starts to form, and that is when we may be onto something.

Medusa is a guardian, she cares for Athena, her temple, and by extension, lives in the service of wisdom, or at least perceives herself as such. It is possible that she has wisdom in her care, or at least by proxy, and when she tends to the temple of Athena, she cares for wisdom. Caring for wisdom does not confer us capability in executing our duties, however, although many of us presume such things. Medusa is a maiden, an unmarried woman, and this implied inexperience and naivety places her precisely in the crosshairs of corruption while pursuing what she believes is a righteous path.

The Greek gods are embodiments of recognizable features of human existence, whether they be emotions, concepts, or personifications of the natural world. They are as untenable as nature itself, and equally forces to be reckoned with. They are asymptotes, which has become a modern analytical geometry term, and comes from the Greek word *asumptotos* (not falling together), and was originally coined by Apollonius of Perga, an ancient Greek astronomer, to describe any line that does not intersect with a given curve. Our lives may twist, turn, and curve, but the gap between us and the gods may only disappear as we approach infinity. Ambition drives us just as easily as naivety, and when these coalesce, we will soon become acquainted with the limits of our wisdom, yet unlikely to recognize its face.

To demonstrate to both ourselves and others that we are true to our cause, we must sacrifice something, and in exchange for this sacrifice, we hope that we will earn something of greater value than what we have offered. Hope is a gamble though, and when humanity is involved, the odds can be difficult to predict; nothing ventured, nothing gained, I suppose. If we have any chance of closing the gap between us and that towards which we've oriented ourselves, in this case, wisdom personified as Athena, payment is due, and Medusa swore an oath to hold nothing above Athena. Her sacrifice was to be demonstrated by maintaining the purity of her dedication by remaining celibate.

Celibacy is a somewhat contentious concept, and one that seems to have fallen out of favour in the modern world to a large extent due to the popular correlation between sexual liberty, semi-hedonistic proclivities, and women's rights. It's not that these aren't legitimate expressions of individualistic sovereignty, but somehow conversations regarding restraining human impulses or desires are few and far between now. It's as if the antithetical claims for discipline, patience, and worth have been dispensed with for some reason greater than their inconvenience. One perspective is that sexual liberty has value that is defined in a manner directly opposed to celibacy, but I don't believe it works out quite like this. They seem to me to have concordant value, and they can both be applied simultaneously if the approach is well-measured.

This is somewhat of a digression, but I think it's worth appreciating that sexual conduct is another subject that we believe we've worked out to the extent that it isn't discussed openly very much anymore, and it has largely been replaced with advertising and pornography that serve as education for such things as if these were accurate depictions of healthy human relations. Essentially, I think we should talk about sex more often publicly, not in specific terms, but at least topically in a helpful and constructive manner. Regardless, to relinquish a freedom, particularly one with such potent pressures, is to sacrifice something of significant value. The problem here for Medusa, however, is that she may not possess the constitution to preserve such a thing, and even if she did, it may not be something she is capable of relinquishing free of interdiction.

Despite any criticisms that may be levied against individual humans, I am strongly committed to the notion that every human has value, both intrinsically, that we obtain by virtue of our birth, and through what may constitute unrealized potential. I am equally committed to the notion that despite such claimed foundational value that each of us possess, the uniformity likely ends there, as our value varies so greatly both in sort and application that it may be impossible to compare them in most situations. I find it strange that it seems almost a sin to point out in the modern era that despite each of us having value, some are capable of producing more than others, and despite unrealized potential, some of us actively generate more value than others. This isn't meant to diminish any of our values, but it is clear that regardless of where the foundation lies, some ceilings are far higher than others, even if we were to consider variance in sort as equally valuable.

There is no doubt that Medusa has value, which is why she is described as possessing flowing golden locks, worn upon the head, like a crown. In literature, whether it be by composition or translation, how things are described is relevant, and the precision with which something is described offers insight into their importance. Medusa having blonde hair is one thing, to have it described as golden is another, and to modify what could've otherwise been straight or plain hair and give it character, such as curls or ringlets, is to insist that we notice such a thing. Medusa, the maiden with flowing golden locks, elicits something very different than Medusa, the girl with the blonde hair. She has value, illustrated through hair of great material worth, with a shape similar to coins, or perhaps it is a pattern that feeds back into itself, like infinity, or ouroboros, a snake swallowing its own tail, representing rebirth. Despite any hair or symbolism regarding it, it is clear she has value, because she caught the eye of Poseidon, god of the sea, brother to Zeus, the king of the gods. When an entity is so powerful that they may bed any they choose, whom they select is likely to infer worthiness.

Seduce and Shackle

There is a contested matter to examine now, which is the seduction of Medusa by Poseidon. *Seduction* is the resulting word in most translations, however there are many framings of this interaction that may dramatically alter our understanding of these events, although the outcome does not change. Was this a relationship between the two? Did Poseidon mislead her with his words and was she tricked into some sort of arrangement? Can such a situation exist where an authentic connection is even possible? In many western nations, if someone in a position of authority attempts to make an advance on a subordinate in the workplace, depending on how it is gone about, this may constitute sexual assault, because the context implies that there may be consequences, conspicuous or otherwise, that a failure to perform some favour, commit to a relationship, or cease an existing one, may result in career sabotage. Can any human meet a god and be immune to the imposition of their status? Perhaps, but it is unlikely that total immunity is an option, whether it be fear, awe, or attraction that may compromise our will. Meeting powerful people or someone we idolize is one thing, but meeting a god is another. Worse still, perhaps it is unapologetic and unambiguous rape, where Medusa is a victim of a very particular sort: a plaything of the gods absent any care or concern for her humanity.

Whether she is a lover, a partner, a fling, or a victim doesn't really seem to change the naivety on display. We seem expected to perceive her as a victim of circumstance, but one that is only possible due to her immaturity. Regardless of her characterization, she is certainly in over her head, even as a maiden who genuinely pursues wisdom in the bosom of a goddess. I don't believe that the particulars of the *seduction* are ultimately relevant, which many may find unacceptable, if my research on the topic is any indication. Without a doubt, the victimization of Medusa seems to be the prominent focus of bloggers, journalists, and special interests that, in my estimation, can't see the forest for the trees. If your goal is to maximize interest and allegiance through victimhood narratives, this would certainly be the story element to highlight, but it fails miserably at respecting what the reader may glean from exposure to the complete picture in favour of an agenda or what I suspect may be confession through projection. Medusa is unequivocally a victim in the story, but I believe the best way to characterize her status while respecting the importance of archetypal themes is to recognize she is caught in the tangle of powers beyond her control that exist solely to serve those that reign. We can be well-intentioned, in the pursuit of wisdom, in the service of the gods, and yet we may find ourselves inevitably staring down the barrel of a gun if we have misread the landscape. Despite effort or intention, maps never match their territory, they serve us only as a guide with utility in mind and nothing else.

Regardless of how you would like to characterize the seduction, to the surprise of none, it was discovered by Athena. She is, after all, the goddess of wisdom, and although the gods were notorious for both their indiscretions and their inability to effectively conceal them, these events are taking place in the temple of a goddess defined by her capacity to see and know all. The circumstances, as unfortunate as they may be, have placed Medusa in the crosshairs of Athena, who shares much more allegiance with her kin, Poseidon. Indiscretions are to be punished by the gods, and even if Poseidon was wholly responsible for this violation, it will always be preferable to punish the mortal and keep relations between fellow gods friendly. This is largely why it makes no difference how we characterize the seduction, because regardless of who is responsible, Athena will see no other option than to punish Medusa, a deduction that we see on display with some regularity in our own lives. People look after their own, even if it would be immoral, and taking issue with it isn't likely to offend the conscienceless.

Punishment isn't often dispensed in a manner that we perceive as justice, especially when it's directed at us. Let's consider the dilemma Medusa faces: Poseidon is in a position of authority, he is a god, and this places Medusa in jeopardy. Either she rejects the advances of Poseidon, or she violates her covenant with Athena. There is no reason to believe that Poseidon would even acquiesce to her denial of his company, the gods aren't known for being honourable or respectful. Athena demonstrates her proclivity as a god to punish the mortal. Humans are chess pieces, after all, to be moved on the board as they see fit, worthy of being sacrificed in the pursuit of power and pleasure. Life isn't fair, but it could be that disavowing the favour of the god of wisdom would be a worse choice than denying the god of the sea, if the choice were even available.

Punishment seems to be inherent to wisdom, not that it is ever capable of dealing it directly. Rather, when we behave in an unwise manner, we are likely to be punished for it, and sometimes we should be. Wisdom personified, or in this case, deified, needs to punish someone for an unwise act, and although it may present as an act of anger or retribution in this case, it serves to demonstrate that if you disobey wisdom, there will be suffering. As a result, thematically speaking, being punished by Athena doesn't have the same meaning as being punished by another god. There is something to be appreciated that Medusa devoted herself to wisdom, and when she found herself involved in breach of her covenant with the goddess of wisdom, it is precisely wisdom that convicted her. It doesn't make it fair, especially if we interpret the seduction to be a vicious attack, but stories that survive the ages do so because they resonate with us, and it doesn't seem as if existence and fairness are on speaking terms most of the time.

The punishment crafted by the hands of wisdom is both poetic and destructive, as is characteristic for themes that cause the archetypal heart to beat. Athena turns Medusa's golden locks into snakes, and causes her gaze to turn any living thing to stone, twists of fate that compel both sympathy and awe. Let's start with the new hairstyle.

Swallowing Snakes

Medusa has been robbed of her value-defining feature in the story, but this isn't to infer she is valueless, she is simply taking on a different role in the second act. Gold is golden and snakes slither and hiss, but in this story, they aren't too different. Gold is precious, and to whatever we ascribe worth will inevitably be coveted, but that which is coveted is only sought because of what may be done with it. Whether it is spent or saved, we amass wealth because of its power to purchase and convert. Ideally it would magically appear in our hands, but generally it requires some amount of effort to obtain, such as work, sales, theft, or investment. We willingly exchange goods and services for money because it permits us with the opportunity to convert our efforts into anything of our choosing, provided we have sufficient funds. Alchemists famously attempted to turn lead into gold, but the reason why this would even be considered a worthwhile endeavour is because of what may be done with gold; if it had no power to purchase things, then no one would bother. The underlying premise here is that gold is valuable because it unlocks potential. It is accumulated through specificity, and it can be spent with specificity, but for the time it is in our possession, we wield generalized power, that is, the ability to choose its path. This is a literal conjugation of course, and it is one we see in every monetary transaction, from a chocolate bar to a house, but in the story, her golden locks are a symbol of the value gold provides. She isn't trading it for wine or pistachios, or whatever a maiden in ancient Greece would want. This is why I would describe the transition from golden locks to snakes as more of a lateral move than a demotion.

In stories, snakes are a symbol of fertility and rebirth, and in this story, it is no different. While some may find this evident, it is often lost on many because snakes are one of the more popular primal fears we possess, and as a result, a crown of snakes would sooner evoke a shiver than intrigue. Snakes shed their skin through *sloughing*, which is to remove or shed something no longer needed, and it is for this reason that they symbolize transformation. When Athena takes something of value from Medusa, she replaces it with a canonical symbol of rebirth, and she becomes an entity that contains a potential that may be unlocked. The literal rebirth from maiden to monster is clear, but the manifest foreshadowing is palpable when we consider the remainder of the story. While our inclinations may be to perceive this transformation from beauty to beast as a diminishing of her worth, it can be plausibly concluded that a transaction has occurred, exchanging one symbol of potential for another, and it could be argued that the enigmatic aftermath possesses a greater respect for the complexity of human existence. The stone-gaze is another matter entirely, and one deserving of a particular standard of respect that I hope I can meet.

Eyes On Us

Humans have a particular interest in eyes, we always have, and they have garnered their fair share of aesthetic attention in literature, philosophy, and poetry. Additionally, their complex structure and functionality have drawn numerous disciplines into their orbit, including evolutionary biology, medicine, and forensics. Few body parts, aside from human genitalia, with which we seem particularly preoccupied, have found their way into so many niches.

Our eyes are very sensitive, and we are very sensitive about them. When I am delivering a first aid course, my mere utterance of the term *extruded eyeball* typically earns me a few shivers and grimaces, and when the cartoon depiction of the injury is on-screen, there is at least one participant that looks away until I change the slide. Eye injuries make us squeamish, and when one stray lash that was once conspicuously perched nearby makes contact with our lens, it becomes a matter of life and death to remove it.

Besides objective considerations, there is the matter of what they provide us: sight, and any experience we have that extends from this. Being able to see is predominantly just a preamble, and one we take for granted, because we never consider thanking our sight for the experiences made possible by its companionship. In fact, it would be weird to thank eyes for anything, because the sight produced by our eyes and made coherent by our brain are both part of us, right? Wouldn't I just be thanking myself? That's stupid. Perhaps, but you could engage in a compelling introspection about what constitutes the self, and it isn't unreasonable to deduce that consciousness is an emergent phenomenon made possible by the brain. That being said, even if they weren't, it's not as if your body parts could comprehend praise without their own respective consciousness. Now that I've just provided you with something that you can ponder the next time that you're on drugs, I'll move on.

There are many visual experiences that give us pause, and we tend to list them among our favourites. The exchange of immersive facial scans that follow an unanticipated kiss that leads to another, the first time you cradle your newborn and lovingly gaze at him or her, taking in a quiet and starry night on a lake when everything is still, the potency of these cannot be denied. Not all of these would appeal to everyone, but I believe we're speaking the same language. There is something unusual about the stone-gaze of Medusa though, and this is where the severity of the punishment for behaving in a manner antithetical to wisdom presents itself.

Gorgon Is as Gorgon Does

"Maybe now you can stop the movement of man,
and render them inanimate."

This appears to be the sentiment of Athena's twisted gift, the newly acquired trait of Medusa, powerful and burdensome. Some care was taken in crafting the particulars of how this gift is expressed, which infers some amount of control over whom it can be directed towards. While a reduction in the unwieldiness of a weapon would generally make it more attractive, this particular weapon cuts deep in both directions. Anyone can observe Medusa without concern, and she can observe others in kind, but if the boundaries of the peripheral are trespassed by the wanton desires of both parties, the visual approximation of an authentic exchange ceases immediately following its creation; one becomes the calm, the other the storm. Any care for the soul that may have materialized crashes prior to flight.

Somewhat sinister, isn't it? Even if Medusa was complicit in her affair and therefore fairly convicted of her tortious breach, is this the punishment due? If we consider redemption a concept worth pursuing, would it be achievable in the face of a carefully crafted punishment that eliminates the potential for a connection only made possible through a beating heart behind human eyes? Can a scorned social animal that yearns for the company that cures loneliness be rehabilitated from such a state without the reciprocity of earnest love? Unlikely, but perhaps Athena has other pieces on the chessboard in mind, with intentions of sacrificing Medusa for the crowning of another.

With the erosion of potential intimacy likely taking hold, what can be expected of a maiden-turned-monster? I am not willing to do an assessment on the expectations that may fall amidst the tension of free will at this time, as it would require its own book to do it any justice, but I believe that it is at least fair to ascribe some amount predictive value to what may occur. Medusa, once a maiden and now a monster in form, will have her essence follow its lead in due time. It isn't necessary for this to be the case, but in the absence of an epiphany or external intervention, the odds should encourage a wager.

Regardless of her guilt or innocence, and whether she likes it or not, Medusa now serves another purpose, as both a means and an end. This may not be desirable, but it isn't without merit. Not everyone can shine as bright as the heavens, despite our innate competitive drive and desire for resources, and I believe that the mechanisms that propel others forward to greatness are no less great than the brightest star in the sky. Some believe that everyone wants greatness as much as they do, but the humble exist among us, and their love for unlocking potential in others is no less fulfilling for them. Like any teacher worth their pay, their joy should flow forth from the moments when students have academic breakthroughs and reach a new level of personal proficiency. Their students may become even greater than them, but the teacher is no less impor-tant in the scheme than the star. This is why my current view of the quality of Western teachers and education is so disheartening, because ideological progressivism, political agendas, and summers off seem to have been sufficient enough tokens to rob youth of their futures. Western academics no longer appear interested in assisting youth shape themselves, they seek to shape them in their own image, gods reigning over a realm of lost souls.

While a rose-coloured view of Medusa's transformation may be placative, it doesn't reasonably address the turmoil she experiences, and she isn't likely to concede her hopes and dreams and dispense with her suffering due to an acknowledgement of her shift from actor to conveyance. I will not pretend that this is fair, or absolve justice and infer that she just needs to accept it, but please remember that this is a story, and its purpose is to offer insight into humanity and our circumstances. Stories can serve as either warnings or guides, and whichever you believe is more appropriate will likely be dictated by the state of your perception when you consume it. I will not defend Medusa's victimhood because she requires no counsel; she is an archetype, not a person.

If someone finds themselves in a situation similar to that of Medusa, then depending on the details, I may be inclined to weigh in, but to suffer through defending why a story character requires justice is to impose yourself on the story. Our perception doesn't sufficiently serve as an interface for communication when archetypes are concerned. There is certainly some amount of us embedded in the process of constructing the story, but the reason that some things are archetypal and others not appears to be an emergent phenomenon. We don't dictate archetypes; we recognize them after witnessing their imposing visage.

Even when Jung was trying to give shape to archetypes, he wasn't creating or establishing them; he was giving them definition so that we may better understand what we find so resonant when we may have previously lacked the helpful characterizations or language to do so. Jung didn't create anything, he clarified them for us. We can receive insight about ourselves from archetypes, but we don't create them, and to inject ourselves into an archetype is to travel down a path that leads to an intellectual and spiritual dead end. This isn't simple or obvious, clearly, but for now, I would recommend avoiding personifying yourself as an archetype. We may recognize them in ourselves, but we are far more than what any of them offer on their own. To personify an archetype is to dramatically oversimply human existence and reduce it to a caricature of our complexity; we are more than that, and we deserve more than that.

Fear and Humanity

No longer a servant of wisdom, Medusa flees the temple of Athena, a twisted creature that both embodies and serves a new master: fear. In this moment, robbed of her purity, innocence, and, in some way, her value, she hastily retreats to somewhere safe, scrambling until she can settle for a moment, but no such place exists. The only suitable place would be somewhere where solitude reigns supreme, the furthest place possible, beyond the gaze of man and those wretched gods. She travels to the island of Sarpedon, the end of the earth, the only place that can serve as a sanctuary, as the blind pose no threat to Medusa, and are themselves immune to her power. It is here she spares others from her horror, while conspicuously concealing it. She can hide in plain sight.

The horror of Medusa is a hydra, a serpentine beast with many heads, each capable of swallowing a different part of her humanity. Our conscious and present experience that locks us in place when we gaze into the eyes of another, if only for a moment that precedes fawning or ferocity, is memorable indeed, authentic and connective. This moment, a repeatable and enjoyable experience that we seek out when the opportunity presents itself, will forever elude Medusa. If she were to participate in such an exchange, she would render them immobile, and destroy the future of a mind that would otherwise be capable of reminiscing. Her love makes life stand still, while the soul of the victim dissipates, and what remains is a memory incapable of remembering anything. Her horror is connection defined by care.

Whatever remained of Medusa's humanity after her transformation cannot be expected to last. What happens to a human that is no longer able to connect with humanity? What is a human without their humanity? Is it considered a human trait to be capable of losing your humanity? Where does it go? Despite any conceptual wordplay, Medusa did not start off as a monster, but she becomes one by the end. The inevitability of an inability to connect with humanity offers a relief of the conscience, and an existence defined by resentment. To be consumed by victimhood swallows everything else along with it, and without virtues, all conduct is justified as recompense.

Medusa cannot gaze upon herself; her power is so terrible that she cannot face herself and continue to live in this victim manifestation. Humans have a capacity for denial that can be requisitely met should the need arise for offense or defense. Whether this exists as a survival mechanism or as a limitation of a state of existence is unclear; regardless, human history is littered with countless examples of victim-fueled retaliatory conduct, perceived to be perfectly justified in the mind of the duplicitous victim.

A large part of how we can earnestly victimize others, besides being absent conscience, is our insistence that we are never attacking, we are only ever defending. We will no longer tolerate being victimized, and we will chain ourselves to the trees of our convictions, immobile and insolent. Medusa, the devouring mother, is therefore justified in the reign over her island, the mobility of the blind is stagnant, and a landscape of stasis establishes itself. The only company she may keep are the blind, and they are unaware of the threatening creature that lurks in their proximity. Those without vision can coexist with Medusa, blind to what she is, and can live out their days in peace with the intrinsic limitation imposed on them, forever unaware of what they could become if they were able to break free from their blindness. It is among the blind where Medusa feels safe, incapable of turning anyone to stone, but simultaneously capable of reigning over them should she see fit. She is advantaged only in a settlement of the sightless.

The Feedback Loop of Imitation

The parallels between this mythical living arrangement and reality are quite clear. It isn't entirely accurate to describe this as life imitating art, however, because archetypal themes are woven into human existence both in structure and substance. It isn't as simple as one imitating the other, rather they are part of a feedback loop, and they shape one another over time through iterative processes of expression, recognition, and reflection.

If we were to dramatically oversimplify the devouring mother archetype, strip down the mythos, and convert it into a crude human product, it retains its relevance and resonance, which is arguably an indication of its truth; its utility does not diminish with a change in resolution. A common feature of a population that becomes increasingly wealthy over generations is that parents become increasingly co-dependent in tandem.

A typical offering from the hearts of parents is that they want their children to have *more* than they did when they were children, and generally speaking, they would like them to suffer *less*. There are two major problems with this approach, however, despite its concurrence of perceived categorical benevolence. First, if an increasingly wealthy population continues this trend over generations, then at which point do the children become spoiled? If a parent never had toys as a child, and as such they desire a simple carved wooden car for their child, this is one step up by comparison to their respective child-hood. If the child with the wooden car becomes a parent one day, they may similarly desire more for their child, and this may present as a more sophisticated toy car, whether this is reflected in the cost, features, or branding. It doesn't need to be a toy or a car obviously, it can be whatever is one iterative step up from the perceived recollection of the parent. If this trend continues, as it tends to for many aspiring parents seeking to fill the perceived gaps of their upbringing through gesture and gift, and a generalized increase in wealth is present, then successive generations will want for so little, they may begin to perceive that anything less than the apex of luxury constitutes justified discomfort and dissatisfaction. The child that once both happily and humbly accepted a minor token of material love will become the great-grandparent of the child that spits and punches if they have their one-thousand-dollar cellular device taken from them temporarily.

The second problem is that this phenomenon doesn't exist in a vacuum. Humans are social animals and we are keenly interested in both the states of existence and performativity of our neighbours. These inclinations will become supercharged due to the same sorts of parents doing everything they can to ensure that their child won't be singled out for having less than whatever is expected to be the norm amongst peers. Before you know it, children who have never known anything resembling destitution will perceive an insufficient number of worshipping subjects as an existential crisis, as social media has generously informed us. I don't believe that there is anyone or any-thing to blame for this, it seems to me that it may just be a sign of the times. That being said, while the general circumstances may be a force of nature, to pretend that individual parents lack agency is to provide an excuse that is both untenable and unhelpful. Whether it is learning to tie your shoe laces, riding a bike, driving a car, or climbing to the highest branch on the tree, we have all experienced the transformative nature of personal accomplishment; it is a human truth. This, however, appears to have been confused with reckless-ness, bother, or suffering, and as a result, the parent that wants more for their child saves them from any and all discomfort and in doing so, consumes the seeds of growth and potential. The devouring mother always hungers, and her love demands bondage.

I am combining somewhat distinct situations here. My intention isn't to conflate archetypal sin with technological progress, rather, I am simply making an analogy in an attempt to argue that progress over time may serve as a factor in an exaggerated manifestation of particular archetypes. I am hypothesizing that a decrease of existen-tially challenging factors, and the meaning and fulfillment we obtain from their conquer, invokes in us a compensatory pressure to find meaning through other means. This may include an inclination, des-perate or measured, conscious or not, to impede on the progress of others so that we may be needed, or loved.

Parents are the low-hanging fruit for this serpentine sin, and so they made for an easy analogy, but if you recall, I stated that embody-ing the devouring mother was *my* sin; I may be casting stones, but I have reserved a supply for myself. Self-flagellation is pathetic and unbecoming, but there is value in the odd stone cast, regard-less of whom it may be directed at; it keeps us honest. Regardless of the victim, to devour competence or potential through interven-tion, placation, or a sense of duty, we are encouraging dependence and discouraging independence. Our care begets horror, our love begets statis.

Beneath the veil of justifications and perceived righteousness lies a desperate heart in search of an anchor, but how are we to recog-nize this in others or ourselves? Are there recognizable differences between authentic love and its reflection? What is authentic love? What is love? Baby, don't hurt me . . . because I'll be covering those in the last part of the book. For now, I will transition to Perseus, and place focus on his journey that ultimately leads to the clash of these archetypal titans. I abstained from elucidating too much on Perseus in my earlier breakdown of the story, so I will shed some light on his origins now to provide a more detailed understanding of what I meant by him having his own sordid tale of deceit and revenge.

Perseus, Son of Zeus

It was prophesied that a future heir to the throne of Argos would kill and replace the current king, Acrisius. Once he became aware of this prophesy, he locked away his only daughter, Danae, in a bronze chamber or tower, depending on the version. Men were kept away from her to prevent a pregnancy, and by extension the birth of this foretold heir. Even in stories, fear and a desire to retain power cause humans to do extraordinary things, it seems. The gods become somewhat irritated when a mortal attempts to interfere with their edicts in a manner similar to when the powerful among us find ways of coercing and punishing us for the crime of free thought and action. Additionally, the gods were known for their inability to abstain from engaging in sexual conduct with mortals, and this story is no exception. Zeus desired Danae, and he made his way into her chamber as a golden rain (or mist) and into her womb, impregnating her, unbeknownst to Acrisius. The Greeks were virgin birth hipsters; they did it before it was cool.

After Perseus was born, and Acrisius discovered the baby was male, he locked Danae and Perseus in a wooden chest, and cast them into the sea, believing that he had rid himself of his heir and triumphed against the gods. Fate is a strange thing however, and some things appear to be immune from interference, despite our best and most desperate efforts. Zeus' brother and God of the sea, Poseidon, calmed the waters and the chest washed up on the shore of Seriphos, where they were taken in by Dictys, who cared for them and raised Perseus to manhood. Dictys was the brother of King Polydectes, however, who had become enamoured with Danae, and he perceived Perseus as an obstacle. Perseus had grown into a strong and honest man, and he was very protective of his mother, and so Polydectes took steps to remove him from the picture.

There is a complex game of fortune taking place here. Danae was imprisoned and dehumanized due to misfortune, but then conceived and birthed a noble and dedicated son, and managed to survive being cast into the sea due to good fortune. She had escaped the grasp of one king and now finds herself in the tangled web of another. Perseus survived a murder attempt by one king, and now to finds himself again as the target of another. The ebb and flow of fortune has a will of its own in the minds of mortals, but it is the will of the gods that conducts the orchestra. Polydectes isn't as brash as Acrisius though, he hatched a scheme to eliminate Perseus rather than make an attempt on his life directly. As recompense for the failure to respectfully produce a gift for attending a wedding hosted by Polydectes, and despite this obligation being concealed from

Perseus, he offered to give anything the king desired; Polydectes requested the head of Medusa.

The dangers of retrieving such a gift are obvious, but when you've been embarrassed publicly at a wedding hosted by the king, you don't have much of a choice. The show must go on, as it is said, and this trickery is the mechanism through which the heroic journey materializes. In the absence of deception, would anyone dare travel to the end of the earth and confront the horrible Medusa? While it may be preferable to arbitrate every decision entirely on your own, sometimes we need a little push to confront that which may devour our existence.

Medusa and her infamy as the devouring mother archetype are well-known, and if this is the case, which I believe is mostly salient, then Perseus would be the hero. To be the hero is to be burdened with a challenge that you're expected to accept regardless of how it is initiated. You can live comfortably denying yourself such a burden, but then you wouldn't be the hero, perhaps not something lesser than others, but less than what you could be. The implication being that in order to unlock your potential, you need to adopt a burden of sufficient enough weight that it will activate your call to adventure, and if you succeed, you become a version of yourself that would be otherwise unattainable. This isn't even remotely mysterious once it has been articulated, even if it's the first time you've encountered such a concept. It seems obvious, doesn't it? It's like trying to convince someone that practice makes perfect. Regardless of any existing talent or skill, practicing will either develop or hone proficiency.

As a young man, I never enjoyed baseball practice, but I really enjoyed the games themselves, a common perspective among children and adolescents. I generally didn't care too much for winning the games, but many of my teammates did, and attending practice to improve both your individual and collective proficiencies is a reliable strategy. The relationship between development and achievement isn't a uniquely human dynamic either, it is a fundamental feature of all known organisms. Evolution is a competitive process, so it shouldn't be surprising that organisms that adapt well to the challenges of their circumstances often possess the best chances of successfully procreating. Challenges are the catalyst for improvement; they are the keys to unlocking potential. The greater the challenge, the greater the potential that may be unlocked.

Polydectes believed that this challenge would result in the death of Perseus, but fortune is unpredictable, and if you confront a specific person with a specific problem, it may awaken in them a strength capable of stifling any preconceived notions you have regarding the brilliance of your scheme. In the story, Perseus is half-god, unbeknownst to Polydectes, and he is destined to kill the king of Argos; the bliss of ignorance is only ever palliative, it isn't productive. While Perseus may be capable of more than anyone anticipates, he doesn't miraculously obtain special powers, at least, not without the assistance of the gods. While it may be a matter of individual proclivity that dictates the human inclination to confront such a horrible monster even with the assistance of the gods, it is for many the difference between living and existing, and not just any life, but one worth living.

Perseus had been destined to kill the king of Argos, which infers he has future challenges ahead, and so to an extent, we presume his success in retrieving the head of Medusa. This begs the question though, what is destiny? Is it the same as fate? Is it real? Does destiny have any coherence absent God or gods? Can this coherence be articulated in a manner distinct from ego or confidence? Perhaps, but despite any concrete answers, they've become particularly preoccupied with Perseus and his success. We will examine their interventions to manifest destiny, and see how these fare as a proxy for destiny in our lives beyond the book.

Divine Intervention

Suffice it to say, we are not created equal, and despite any offense taken by these words, their truth persists. This isn't an argument regarding ethics, representation, or fundamental liberty; in these ways, people are equal, despite the contents of our minds being open for debate. There are things that I can do that you cannot, and there are things that you can do that I cannot. This isn't controversial, generally speaking, but it begins to harbour discomfort when we begin the discuss the value that is attributable to our respective talents. We all want to possess skills or talents that are valued, and the more ambitious among us desire those that are valued most, but that doesn't mean it plays out that way. Context heavily influences what is valued, whether it is the market, culture, the time, the place, the stakeholders, and a litany of other uncontrollable elements that dictate worth.

The controversy expands broadly when we begin to assess whether individuals possess the opportunity to capitalize on these skills or talents as a result of systemic influences, or through their own dedication and ingenuity. People have very strong opinions on the subject, most of which aren't particularly useful in developing a functional model that we can implement into our lives. You can desire humans to be wholly social, but we do not live our lives in pure concordance, and we all encounter numerous situations within which we have to choose the path for ourselves. So then, it would behoof us to identify both our strengths and weaknesses, and what can be done with them, if anything. You can wish to be one way or another, but happiness and contentment are only found when you've identified the parameters of yourself and drawn a map on how to navigate them. In this way, life is both perfectly fair and unfair, or perhaps fairness isn't a relevant concept regarding the hands we've been dealt; we must simply play them to the best of our ability.

But who, or what, deals these cards? The answer is functionally very straightforward, but incredibly complex and mysterious conceptually, which is: nothing, in particular. There cannot be a *whom* to which we attribute credit or blame and have it be coherent, that is, unless you support the human proclivity to justify both our greed and our wrath as authentic representations of divine intervention. The incoherence of this becomes immediately clear when you attempt to find reference points to illuminate the validity of these claims, and only ubiquity or ideology follows. At some point you're likely to notice that some don't simply believe themselves touched by God, but rather that they are God; Nietzsche was right. This doesn't mean that I can deduce that this is true or false, rather, that if it is true for one, it must be true for everyone, and if it's false, so than shall it be false for everyone, and then postmodern dictates soon follow, in their perfectly imperfect gnostic nihilism. This is why it isn't functionally useful, if we are to be intellectually honest or consistent, to universalize the genesis of our talents to one or more invisible hands, unless you possess an affinity for presumption and power games.

If there is no useful *whom* to which we can credit with our talents and shortcomings, may there be a *what*? There can be, but this is where mystery and complexity would start to colour and shape the concept with a confounding allure. The complexity consists of a pantheon of deeply rich concepts, each respectively complex in their own right. Among these include a coalescence of genetics and epigenetics, neurobiology, social and psychosocial interactions, personality, any individual deviations, and the context within which these are expressed. The mystery consists of both the known and unknown gaps in these bodies of knowledge, and why they function at all in the way that they do. Human existence has never been understood well enough to satisfy anyone that cared enough to know the truth, yet here we are. To be human, at least for now, is to remain in the dark about why or how anything functions or exists in the way that it does, or if these even have answers; perhaps things just *are*.

Ultimately, it doesn't seem to matter if we understand these things, and in our personal lives, the answer seems only to offer justification or solace. Whatever the case may be, we still need to live, and if you spend your time combatting a reality that extends from a system no one understands, you're either a grifter, or you're lost. The gods in the story may be real or unreal, but they act as the genesis of capability, and they give gifts and dispense punishment as they see fit, whether their reasons are known or unknown by the mortals who remain caught in the tangle. Perseus, son of Zeus, yet remaining a mortal, was given divine assistance to aid him in his quest. Gifts, in this instance, represent talents and skills, or whatever would be necessary to succeed in beheading the devouring mother. In the absence of such gifts, some of us remain forever in the maw of a mother, castigated and bound by the love of a twisted soul.

A Gift Unlike Any Other

No gifts will do to overcome that which devours our competence, especially when each of them may be crippled or compromised by the comfort of suffocating solace. Perhaps, some of us aren't destined to break free from the prison of our potential, a truth that disturbs us as individuals, but serves the hierarchy well enough to be left alone. If any of us stand a chance of surviving the softening of our convictions, we need to familiarize ourselves with the tools of our liberation, whether they are innate or imbibed.

I've done a healthier breakdown on each of Perseus' respective gifts on prior occasions, and there may be marginal comparative value to reproduce them here, but I believe they would serve as a distraction in this case, given the specific context within which the story is being examined. While every gift was imparted by deity and divinity alike, and only one chosen by each, there is the one that was given by wisdom incarnate herself, who selected a mirrored shield to assist Perseus in the massacre of the maw.

A plain mirror would possess value in this endeavour, and a dull shield would serve well in its own respect, but it is the synthesis of these tools that highlight a function of wisdom. A mirrored shield is an object that is greater than the sum of its parts, if for no other reason than it is one object and not two. Furthermore, it is not a shield with a mirror crudely stuck to it, it is the sort of alchemical product that only wisdom generally tends to produce; it is a compound contraption. The elegance of a multi-tool is that it embodies in one object what could've only existed once a sufficient amount of knowledge and experience had been accumulated to understand why it would be valuable in the first place. Additionally, a multi-tool is useless to anyone who doesn't do work, an implicit limitation of its value to any individual, but even then, most recognize that it may still come in handy should we ever need to use one, so why not keep one in the house?

Multi-tools are so commonplace in the modern era that it's easy to take them for granted, and it wouldn't be the only thing we overlook in its beauty and elegance due to the way modernity shapes the perception of the living. We often forget that things iterate over time, and it is only with both the knowledge and the experience with the implementation of said knowledge that wisdom can exist. The purpose of iterative processes is to produce a depth of understanding, high-quality discernment, and a capacity for exercising and providing sound judgment, or more simply put: wisdom. Temper this in a forge with ethics and truth, and you can produce something that rivals the gods. Wisdom isn't the only possible product of such knowledge and experience, it just happens to be the only one possible absent a cynical mind, or a psychopathological proclivity.

We are the benefactors of wisdom, and like a spoiled offspring of parents that had to work tirelessly their entire lives to be able to spoil the child, it is easy to perceive our insulated existence as an existential constant, because it is all that we know. Perception may be *our* reality to an extent, but it isn't reality, and to ignore the current and historical realities that persist without concern for how we perceive them is to be in a state of perpetual apathy for anything beyond your own experience, and nihilism is likely to follow. Let's see how that works out for you.

A mirror is an object that permits things to be seen for what they are, and a shield is something to defend against aggression. A shield polished to a mirror finish retains the utility of both, but it is also the perfect object to wield when confronting the sort of aggression that only seeks to defend itself. Against Medusa, the mirror is strategic, permitting Perseus to approach her without looking at her directly, so he can avoid being turned to stone. Against any devouring mother, it is symbolic of the same thing: a strategic approach that permits us to get close to her without locking eyes and witnessing her humanity, lest we lose our nerve to break free from our bondage in lieu of breaking her heart.

In truth, in order for any devourer to cease their consumption, their nature needs to be cast back onto them, so they can see themselves for what they are, and this needs to be done by one of their victims, who has gathered enough will not only to confront the horror, but enough to demand a life that may be shaped by their own hands. We seem perpetually confused about what freedom means, as if this concept makes any sense within a context of stasis. You may claim that you are freely living as a statue, of your own avail, and I would claim that you don't know what *living* means. I would support a revolution of the self, without condoning any misguided interpretations of my writing to be a wholesale support of a larger-scale revolution, as these often have their own mothers, who willingly devour their followers in the pursuit of generally predictable ideological outcomes.

It may be considered cowardly to approach a monster indirectly, as some may interpret a stealth assassination as evil, but there are contextual truths that reveal themselves in specific situations. We are in a tough spot however: how do you confront something directly that will stop you in your tracks? It is precisely due to our diminished prowess and competence at the hands of Medusa that prevents us from attacking her directly. Let me remind you that we aren't confronting a real monster, nor are we killing anyone in real life, rather, we are severing a bond of one sort, in an attempt to form one or more in the aftermath. It is easy to permit things to be done for us, especially if we're inclined to be pampered, if we seek reprieve, or if the care is just so good, we believe ourselves foolish to give it up. In fact, we could each construct a paradise from which we would never want to leave, where we are waited on hand and foot, enjoying whatever pleasures we desire; how hard would that be to leave? Well, that depends, I guess.

Breaking the Silence

Without delving too deeply into any psychological or evolutionary principles, the extent of our capacity to make meaning, and by extension happiness, whatever this means, will largely be informed by our peripheral experiences. To be immersed in a state of existence where things seem to serve at our pleasure from birth is to be denied the opportunity to develop competence, and ultimately, a sense of yourself. This is because evolution is a competitive process, and as products of evolution, it should go without saying that we need challenges to overcome in order to flourish. When immersed in a similarly pleasurable existence later in life, after we have developed competence, made achievements, and have earned this state of existence, temporary or permanent, then the same existence becomes a trophy, won through our triumphs. Essentially, achievements give states of existence meaning within their respective context. This is why two identical states of existence can be perceived very differently depending upon their peripheries.

In a similar vein, demanding of competition, however unconcerned with context we are, is one of the fundamental states of human psychology. We don't generally seem to enjoy being at rest all the time, and fulfillment only ever seems temporary. This is consistent with Buddhist traditions, but it's also consistent with speculation made by Dostoevsky about what a potentially idyllic existence would result in, if humans were to ever achieve such a state. He argued that if we were to live an existence completely free of war, and that there was enough wealth around to give everyone every earthly pleasure we desired, from luxurious food and drinks to entertainment and company, and that we never needed to do anything except enjoy these things for the rest of our days, that even then, humans would find a way to disrupt this, if only so that something would happen to shatter this solemnity. You can say what you want about Dostoevsky, but his intimate knowledge of the human condition was so complete that few people in history pose as adequate rivals. He wasn't condemning humanity with his words, not at all, he was simply pointing out that humans seem to *need something to happen*, as if their sanity were predicated on it. It is this psychological compulsion in us that would compel us to scream, just so that we can shatter the silence of a static existence, even one rendered monotone by comfort and guarded by a serpent's coil. You don't know what you're missing, my friend.

A reliable way of parsing between the status of victim and hero within this paradigm is the experience of living and the recognition of its worth. Obtaining this experience is the first step, and even then, the recognition of how to assess or attribute worth to particular journeys is never a guarantee. This requires a whole different set of intuitions and critical thinking, but let's not put the cart before the horse. It is, generally speaking, easier to remain as you are, and abstain from the inertia that sweeps us off our feet and carries us off into uncharted realms. This is why many of us cease to exist in a figurative sense, despite any literal truths on offer. In fact, it may be so difficult for us to confront our devouring mother that we fail in the stages of initiation. We have stability, comfort, and nourishment, and we've heard things about biting the hand that feeds, and although it remains somewhat mysterious, we're comfortable.

We may be comfortable in a general sense, and likely in a relative sense, but being comfortable has never meant being fulfilled, or being happy, or knowing what it's like to perceive the world so clearly that it pierces any crippling doubt that instills the fear of God in you. It is never easy, but if you want to live, it is necessary to move beyond statis, and not just to anywhere nearby, that won't do at all. Jung claimed that *in sterquiliniis invenitur*, in filth it will be found, that is, the thing that you need the most will be found in the place you'd least like to look. We need to travel to the one place that places us at the greatest risk, to confront Medusa herself; we need to travel to the end of the earth.

The End of the Earth

What is established to be a great distance in the story is representative of a measure or mechanism through which you will mortifyingly rebel against the comfort of your existence. Patience is a virtue for a sound mind in apprehension, and courage is a virtue for a frail heart at rest. For profound growth to occur, you need to travel to where you believe the limits reach; nothing ventured, nothing gained. A point worth making is that the limits reach only as far as you can perceive them, but once you've ventured to these limits, the horizon has a peculiar yet unsurprising way of broadening and pushing ever further than you previously believed possible. To many, this may seem like the beginnings of a life riddled with work and unrest, and to an extent, it is. Keep in mind that beheading your devourer has never been a conclusion or a happy ending, it is an invitation to a life wherein you become the shaper of meaning, the God of your own purpose. You can rest along the way once you've started, but do not be mistaken in believing that once you've broken free from your mould that new asymptotes will emerge and beckon you anew. We are all free to abstain from this sort of life, and be pleasantly plump leeches until our death. Be aware, though, that your inability to leave sustenance in your wake will be purposeless and meaningless, and your deathbed delusions may haunt you in your last moment before you enjoy the sweet release of your guiltless existence.

The end of the earth is the last stop after checking everywhere else, our hopes of finding more easily accessible meaning. It is reached as a last resort, and not because you want to be there. It is where you need to go to overcome limitations, because any stop you make prior to the limit will not improve you, because you aren't being tested. It is only the end of the earth, from where you may not return, and where terrible things reside, that can serve as a catalyst for your transformation. When you arrive, and you confront your devourer, it is time to deal the killing blow. I don't generally condone violence, but I am also not a pacifist, and while our inclinations may be to understand our devourer, this isn't the sort of problem that can be resolved through discussion or debate; the devourer needs to be destroyed.

No Head is Better Than One

If you recall my earlier incredulity in purporting that a defense for the death of Medusa is unnecessary, this was stated quite clearly because Medusa is an archetype, and her death doesn't represent the death of a living person. You could say that we are severing *a part* of someone, and I would wholeheartedly agree. The beheading of Medusa is to viciously pursue the wisdom of a life lived freely by acting in a courageous manner for yourself, and out of kindness for her. She may be a victim of one sort, but she has made us a victim of another, and by freeing ourselves from her grasp, we free her from the burden of care for someone that does not want nor need it. The personified devourer can then live a life of their own, with one fewer head on their serpentine body. The absence of this maw will conjure in them a burden that should not be underestimated; it is heavy, hollow, and existentially threatening. This is exactly why we cannot reason with Medusa; her emotions will act as penetrating weaponry that pierce through our better natures right through the heart. *All I ever wanted to do was love and care for you*, she will cry as you confront her, sword in hand. For both of your sakes, you will carefully and consolingly whisper, *you've done enough, it is time to rest.* You must be immune to the dissuading power of her victimhood.

To cut the head off is the only way; to sever one source of power, the mind, from the other, the heart. What remains will produce something far greater than the sum of its parts: a corpse that gives rise to life.

The Beauty in Destruction

Some of the innocuous mechanisms of rebirth are *practice* and *experience*, where the version of yourself that iterates precisely because of these things can be described as *different*, whether we are consciously aware or not. A more poetic, yet no less accurate, mechanism of rebirth is the destruction of an entity and the reconfiguration that ensues in its wake. If everyone were self-aware, conscientious, and inclined towards encouraging the maximizing of human potential, then we would only ever need to destroy a part of ourselves, assuming that a feature of our existence was to self-iterate and never settle for our current version. This isn't human, however, nor am I declaring that it should be, and so, Medusae rarely behead themselves. If they did, half of this book would be unnecessary masturbation in print, something that sufficiently plagues the Humanities and Social Sciences already. As a result, we need to take it upon ourselves to cut our respective cords, so that we may at least receive an invitation to the dance. Conflict and rebirth are common and resonant story themes in virtually every cultural tradition, but this pertains to a war within. It cannot, and should not, be scaled up to a societal or civilizational level under the guise of progress and revolution, which are always myopic, predictable, and idealistic, another thing that sufficiently plagues the Humanities and Social Sciences.

A head with a maw can devour, but no head at all spews forth a future that could never have been realized otherwise. From the severed head of Medusa sprang forth Pegasus and Chrysaor, sons of Poseidon and Medusa; two entities whose birth was only made possible from the decapitation of their mother. In the story, Perseus is obviously a distinct character from these brothers, and despite them being kin, we aren't expected to confuse them with one another. The three become allies in the story, but their translation into reality as representations of growth and potential are quite clear: Perseus is the hero figure, Pegasus is the unlocking of potential, and Chrysaor is maturity and competence. Without belabouring their features and likely insulting your intelligence, I'll do only a minor elaboration.

Often in stories, the importance of why something is a particular way is just as important as why they are not. The beheading of Medusa serves the story just fine; Perseus can collect the head and return without the introduction of these brothers at all, but the story was constructed, iterated, and remains with them included to this day. Additionally, why have them be what they are and not something else? Why not only one brother? Or three? Or seven? And why aren't they both human? Why a winged horse rather than another animal? Why not a honey badger? This may be due to honey badgers being indigenous to a completely different part of the world, and so the likelihood of their entry into an ancient Greek story hovers around zero, either way, *honey badger don't care.* Why is Chrysaor a man in his prime, and not a child on the verge of burgeoning discovery? Or an elderly man, wizened and willing to guide? Simply put, because it doesn't make sense given the archetypes at work in the story.

Stories can be fantastical and magical and untethered from the norms and expectations of our reality, but they still need to make sense. Archetypes help stories make sense, and when a writer understands them, it places them in a league of their own. This is why Tolkien and Rowling will be celebrated forever, and why other authors and screenwriters, who may write exciting material, will be forgotten over time, due to their misunderstanding of what makes a story fundamentally resonant, and therefore, *important* to humans. I've left these names unmentioned to spare the more sensitive and nostalgic among us. The details of what remains as pertinent is important, regardless of whether or not you understand why.

Pegasus is a horse because a horse is a beast of burden: strong, purposeful, resilient, and reliable. He is winged because wings provide flight: freedom from the ground, the opportunity and ability to navigate realms of which terrestrial creatures can only imagine. A winged horse represents the unlocking of potential and the constitution to tread on territories unknown.

Chrysaor is a grown man in his prime because grown men are no longer boys in development, or at least they shouldn't be. A man is mature, strong of body and mind, and it is only a man who is capable of wielding a weapon well, and not just any weapon, but one forged and cast from the same valuable material that his mother donned as precious locks prior to her transformation. A grown man in his prime wielding a golden sword represents maturity and competence, and possesses the ability to cause harm should the need arise.

If we were to encapsulate these characters into attributes, ones that anyone may possess, man or woman alike, they would be qualities that may never be realized while under the protection of a guardian. These are precisely the attributes that will forever remain dormant as the devouring mother feeds on our life force to satisfy the stability of her own fragility, and together, we will remain statues, immobile and lifeless, together forever.

. . . Whoever Fights Monsters

There will always be another monster, and another abyss to stare into, and with each intimate meeting of our respective gazes, we take a part of it with us upon our escape, whether it be a taint or a token. Perseus was charged with returning with the head of Medusa, so this story element is already part of the plot, but it alludes to a transformative quality inherent to many journeys that challenge our courage and sense of self. Having a brush with death changes us, and often in ways that we generally avoid discussing in polite company. We bear an indelible mark of the battle, and although they manifest somewhat differently among us, we keep a part of it with us forever. Retaining the head of Medusa is a terrible burden; it is unwieldy and writhing, easy to fumble and potentially dangerous to even yourself, but carrying this burden makes you formidable, at least to those aware that you possess it. To those who don't, well, we've all witnessed situations where someone underestimated another due to their own hubris. Never underestimate a stranger, and since we're dispensing wisdom, never overestimate your ability to assess strangers; we are far worse judges of character than we tend to believe.

This burden offers something more, however, if you wield it wisely and earnestly: it may be used to slay even greater beasts that may stand between you and your destiny, presuming you are pure of heart and coherent enough to tell the difference. This is exactly what Perseus does, after the long journey back home, carrying this burden across the kingdom.

I believe we've adequately established that the Greek gods had a particularly low threshold for their anger, and even when calm, they seem indifferent to human outcomes, despite the frequency of their interventions. Gods will be gods, I suppose!

Poseidon became angered by the boasting of Cassiopeia about the beauty of Andromeda, and he sent the Cetus to attack her kingdom in retaliation. A potentially worthwhile digression that cannot be done justice in such a short period of time would be on Plato's Realm of Forms, and a narrative framework describing utility and beauty in the corporeal world. I may do my own analysis on this sometime, but for now, any curious readers could read one of the many breakdowns available on the subject.

In this instance, something so beautiful that it rivals the gods cannot be tolerated, regardless of whether the boasting is accurate or not. The Greek gods are ideals deified; from them beauty springs forth, it does not go in reverse. You can approach the ideal, but you are never permitted to challenge the form that informs reality. If the gods are ever perceived as less than a mortal in any way, this may cause cracks to form in the foundation of Olympus, and humans may begin to believe silly things, like living a life independent of godly considerations. Poseidon sent the Cetus not only to remind humanity of their place, but also to destroy the beauty that may threaten the supremacy of the gods and creation, even if the beauty of Andromeda doesn't rival the gods, no one would dare make such claims once they witness this cleansing.

The Colliding Galaxies

Andromeda was destined to marry Perseus, and this is a common archetypal plot theme. There is always a hero and a beautiful maiden in ancient stories, and this is because it traces well within the ritualistic courtship of real men and women. This doesn't need to be the case though; Andromeda is a symbol of something extremely valuable for which you'd be willing to risk your life. She could be a man, or a pile of treasure, an object possessing magical power, a redemptive or cathartic mechanism, or any other thing that we believe worthy of value. The reason that men and women are chosen frequently as heroes and captives is twofold. First, humans are a sexually reproducing species, and the biological torque we experience to reproduce possesses undeniable influence over our thoughts and actions. Second, there is no greater treasure than the love of a partner that we can cherish, and trust, and for which we'd be willing to risk our life. I may be a romantic at heart, but I believe this to be true regardless: there is nothing more valuable to us as individuals than the love of a partner that completes us. Admittedly, it could just be the biological torque speaking, and great sex certainly plays a role, but there seems to be two fundamentally distinct existences: one where you and another have recognized that you are two halves of a whole, bound together by authentic love, and one where you have not.

To the victor go the spoils, or so it is promised if you succeed, and still it persists that nothing ventured, nothing gained. Someone or something as coveted as Andromeda can only be earned by slaying a monster sufficiently powerful enough, whether this monster lies within or without. The Cetus isn't an introductory monster that anyone can defeat; confront it without having developed the proper maturity and competence and you will be crushed. You simply aren't ready yet. A monster like the Cetus can only be defeated if you've previously earned enough self-respect while carrying the burden of a lesser monster with you. Fortunately, Perseus is on his way back to the kingdom, burden in hand, after having slain a lesser monster, which he may use as a weapon should the need arise.

In an attempt to absolve herself of her boasting, and spare her kingdom, Cassiopeia chains Andromeda to a rock at the edge of the realm, in hopes that sacrificing her daughter to the Cetus will appease Poseidon and save her kingdom. To chain someone to a rock is to render them immobile, and in this instance, to be sacrificed as a scapegoat, victimized only by virtue of the circumstance of her beauty from birth. She is the mirror image of Medusa, to be sacrificed in appeasement of the gods, and she will soon be united in the afterlife with her recently deceased bifurcated reflection, Medusa.

Perseus arrives and directs the head of Medusa towards the Cetus, turning it to stone and killing it. The beheading of Medusa is what allows the hero to be born, who wields her horror to overcome ever greater challenges. Without beheading the devouring mother, there is no hero. With the power Perseus obtained from killing Medusa, and keeping part of her with him, she can live on to protect others, and act as a guardian for those in need of protection.

Coherent Constellations

Perseus and Andromeda are married, and the fragments of the Cetus were placed in the stars as a reminder of two things: Perseus' bravery, and a warning against anger and jealousy. In the midst of such conflict and turmoil, a bond is forged. The fragments are the residue of the circumstances coming to a close, and now serve to orient us towards the knowledge obtained in the aftermath of the drama. There are two general lessons learned from this story, absent the particulars of the breakdowns along the way, so let's wrap everything up with a nice little bow.

One is that only the courageous and brave are worthy of the spoils on offer at the end of a long and dangerous journey, even if you were thrust into it. Placing yourself in harm's way and sacrificing properly will give you a chance to do great things, even though you may fail. A life filled with opportunities generated through risks that you voluntarily undertake is worth it.

The second is that courage and sacrifice need to be implemented properly in pursuit of the right goals, and that it is a sin to be motivated by anger or jealousy. The path of the righteous and that of the sinful may appear similar, but there will be no victor at the end of one, only turmoil and emptiness for the sinful and self-righteous.

You may not lose your life following the wrong path, but you may lose your humanity, and give birth to regret.

The fragments of the Cetus, a monster so horrible that it needs to be leashed in the deepest and darkest part of the sea, have now been placed among the stars. Stars have particular value to humans, both in reality and in stories. Their magnificence doesn't seem to diminish with a scientific understanding of their nature or how we engage with them. They are lights in the darkness, orienting points that guide us if we are lost, and a map of the universe, at least from our perspective.

It's funny how perspective can fundamentally alter our understanding of something. We persist through night and day; they're small and can be blocked out of sight by a finger, they lack focus and precision in illuminating things of human importance, and they can be rendered non-existent by a cloudy sky. Of course, none of this is true at all. Stars precede and will succeed us, they're so big that any single star could swallow our planet whole, their directionless light illuminates the entire universe, and it is us that is rendered non-existent to them by a cloudy sky, as if they had any concern for us in the first place. Perspective is funny, isn't it?

Orientation and asymptotes have been a theme throughout this book, as they are part of the synthesis of meaningful stories along with archetypes and their resonant attributes. This isn't a coincidence, we as humans need something towards which to orient ourselves in order to feel the tug of destiny that renders us mobile, but also for these things to be somewhat elusive or replicating. The human need for meaning is an insatiable monster in the face of existential dread. So, it is for the devouring mother as it is for the hero, because these aren't distinct entities. We are an embodied pantheon of complex psychological and physiological truths and mysteries, and we have it in us all to personify any or all of the characters in any story given the right circumstances. If we are feeble or powerless, we can change our circumstances, and if we are formidable and powerful, it begs the question: how is it that you rule?

Z

THE FLORAL FRAMEWORK

———

There is a game with which you may be familiar, it is called *l'effeuiller de Marguerite*, or perhaps you may know it as *she loves me, she loves me not*. The player, having a particular person in mind, plucks a fresh flower and tears off its petals one by one, in hopes of having the final petal predict the favourable outcome of "she loves me!" For those unfamiliar, you begin by tearing the first petal and stating "she loves me," which is then followed by a subsequent petal torn, and stating "she loves me not." This continues, alternating between the two predictions until the last petal is torn from the flower, and whichever prediction is made upon the final tear will inform the player of their fortune. A game for romantics perhaps, but we would all prefer that the object of our affection returns our affections in kind, and the discovery of their absence takes a toll on our comfort and pride.

This game, of course, can be easily won, or lost, depending on your familiarity with flowers. Flowers generally have a predetermined number of petals, and if you pick one with an odd number, you'll win every time, provided you began with *she loves me*. On the contrary, if there are only flowers with an even number of petals in your proximity, then simply changing the starting prediction will produce the favourable outcome. It is a game of fortune, and we often relish opportunities to dictate outcomes that would otherwise elude the influence of our will. It's only a silly game, but it's fun to be God, isn't it? Perhaps and perhaps not, and we can often learn a great deal about someone's character if we examine their desire to control the uncontrollable. Keep your eyes peeled.

There is an ocean between those who enjoy games of fortune, and those who attempt to control their outcomes. It may be fun to play God while tearing petals from a flower, but it can be catastrophic if we insist on controlling the outcomes of anything grander in either scale or sentience. An indication of our maturity is the acceptance of things that exist beyond human influence, and an indication of our wisdom is the acceptance of things that will inevitably be contaminated by any attempts we make to influence them. The clumsy hands of a mortal God may be able to shape incredible things, but they can just an easily generate disaster while being incapable of noticing the difference.

Known Unknowns

There are few guarantees in life, and there are many things that we'd like to change or control if given the chance. Many are perfectly noble, and often the same list is perfectly unattainable, especially when you consider the human inability to balance an incredibly large number of complex systems to produce a desired outcome. I am not a pessimist, far from it, and there is certainly value in attempting to improve the state of some things, but often I notice that there are two persistent human failures that significantly impede on human progress in this realm.

The first is that we seem incapable of recognizing that some frameworks cannot be improved upon. They can be changed and made worse, and they aren't perfect, but they may actually be the best that can be produced, despite their genesis. The second is that we are terrible at accurately predicting the peripheral disturbances and disparities that occur as a result of any change we make to any system. This doesn't mean that we should just accept things for what they are and live a life defined by being inconsequential, rather, that we should exercise caution and iterate responsibly, with minor changes occurring over time in order to identify any ripple effects.

Our personal lives are an entirely different matter, where we have a far greater degree of control, and to the extent that we can exercise agency, we are able to shape things more readily in a manner that will produce more immediate results. This doesn't mean that the same models can't be used in a broad range of scales, but it may be wise to master your proximal universe before attempting grander and broader scales; there is a lot of world beyond your universe.

There have been numerous underlying themes in this book, among which are the human condition, value, truth, authenticity, meaning, potential, love, and the importance of narratives. There were clear digressions, including broader social and political con-texts, as well as personal anecdotes illustrating where I believe I was wanderlust, lacking a respect for the autonomy of others, and igno-rant of the mechanism of maximizing human potential. I did this because I believe that personal failures and suffering are best used as a means to teach others about some of the intrinsic pitfalls of human existence. The strange thing is that this belief may be considered heterodox in some circles, where resentment runs rampant and the best use of personal failures and suffering is to direct it outwards. In these circles, relief experienced by the suffering is done at the expense of others, frequently whoever is the easiest target of the day; stunning and brave, Medusa would be proud.

Context frames virtually every aspect of human interaction; a lack of concern for context is a reliable way of delineating between those who believe themselves common and those that perceive themselves worthy of a crown. Love is no exception, regardless of circumstance, context informs both the legitimacy and authenticity of its representation. Love is a game of fortune in many ways, and the whimsy of *Marguerite* respects this fact despite our acknowledgement that it is unlikely to change our fortune either way. We are all players in the game of love, and frequently we find ourselves as either initiator or recipient of affections, as unpredictable or as unwelcome as they may be.

Shapeless Hearts

I began this book discussing our lack of input in various circumstances within which we find ourselves, many of which are among the most important character-defining influences that we encounter. Do our parents love us? What sort of love is it? Certainly, there is biological relatedness driving much of it, and certain parents will be far more interested in bonding and raising their children than others, but beyond these perfunctory inclinations, we lie in fortune's bed. If it is romantic love, we are often surprised at whom we find ourselves becoming enamoured with, an experience that remains a mystery to many, but is likely well-explained by an understanding of phenotype and pheromone compatibility. Then there are situations where we have become the target of another's love, which is likely more commonly underappreciated by women, as they are predominantly responsible for mate selection in most primate species, humans included. Whether our consciousness emerges in the mind of a man or a woman, or in the body of someone fit for reproduction and all of the selective pressures that accompany it, we are forced to rely on fortune. There are ways of gaming fortune: physical fitness, cosmetics, surgery, presentation of status, and group affiliation are a few of the successful strategies that we rely upon in an attempt to tip the scales.

It is difficult to discuss love without straining its value as a concept, or in its capacity to make us feel whole, and I am not seeking to place any undue strain on the human heart. That being said, it would be helpful if we could find a reliable way to distinguish between productive and destructive contexts of love, without diminishing its potency or allure. Tension is a mainstay of love; in fact, we tend to find it embedded in any meaningful endeavour, but what may materialize amidst the tension is unpredictable. We may be reminded that there is a reason humans fear the unknown: it has the capacity to challenge our comfort. What if we find out that we're not nearly as good as we think we are? I'll shatter that illusion right now and save you some time: you're not. We are never as righteous as we think we are, and it is my belief that one of the reasons we continue to believe this about ourselves is that we've never taken the time to examine ourselves well enough to develop a complete picture, likely because we're afraid of what we may see.

I am not going to breakdown ways of loving one another in any explicit manner, I'm sure there are plenty of books available on the subject already, and I'm not one to masturbate in public. My intention is to assist everyone, myself included, with identifying roads that lead to hell despite our best of intentions. I believe in both the reason and goodness of humanity, but that doesn't mean we aren't susceptible to permitting the angels of our lesser natures guide us in the worship of a mirage. It can be difficult to accurately ascertain our bearings, and often we seem unaware of the ship upon which we are sailing. Richard Feynman and his chalkboard have become famous for the words *what I cannot create, I do not understand*, and I generally tend to apply this standard to myself. I cannot create love, and as a result, I probably don't understand it, but I experience it, and I can recognize it, so it certainly *seems* to exist, and I believe that I am a member of a human race that experiences and recognizes it just as I do. So then, although I admit that I do not understand it, that doesn't mean that I avoid attempts at trying to give it definition, even if we need to eat the elephant one bite at a time.

What is love?

Despite the incredibly large number of confusingly similar and often misattributed quotes regarding love and setting it free, what does this mean? Why would we set something free if we loved it? Wouldn't we want to keep something we love? Well, I suppose that depends on how you believe authentic representations of love are characterized. Experiencing love for someone is completely different than how you choose to demonstrate your love towards them; there seems to be a disturbingly common discordance in this realm, and I am hoping to bring them to a crossroads.

We confuse love with many emotions, and we often describe the combination of attraction, attachment, concern, and dependence as love, but I don't believe this is love, and this is one of the more generous groupings. Informed by our lesser natures, we often confuse a whole manner of conscious experiences with love. Lust isn't love, and neither is desire or infatuation. I may want to bed someone so badly that it causes me to struggle to maintain my composure, but that's not love. Friendship isn't love, and neither is relief or advantage. It's great to have company that alleviates our loneliness, or someone we can depend upon and trust, but that's not love. Commitment isn't love either, whether it is a measure of time, effort, or sensation, and often we commit to people and things because it's easier than facing the horde of horrors that lurk in the unknown shadows of new and unfamiliar paths.

The argument could be made that while I may have listed many human concepts and experiences and claimed that they don't each independently constitute love, perhaps if we combine all of them into a single package, then maybe we've caught a pretty good glimpse of love's true face. Unfortunately, I don't believe so, and although this book isn't the correct venue for a respectful dissection of the concept, there are a few considerations that can assist us in casting some doubt on this face. Love is simply too complicated to reduce it to romantic tropes and relational preferences, because we can love many things in very different ways, but we use the word *love* to describe all of them. We love our husbands and wives, girlfriends and boyfriends, we love our children, parents, siblings, friends and pets, and we have completely different reasons and justifications for why we love them, but we use the same word to describe our feelings towards them. We love our fellow citizens, cultures, countries, and Gods, and although this love is different, many of us feel an emotion so strong that we use the same word to describe them. I am aware that we can make attempts at parsing these various loves in a manner to assist with establishing distinct categories, but this isn't what I'm getting after.

As a philosopher, I am trying to establish what a foundation of love may look like, that is, what might be seen in the overlap of every sort. Is there an archetype for love? A pattern that is woven into every type of connection where the word is appropriate? I am aware of how tall an order this is, because I am essentially trying to convince you that I believe there may be a common theme that runs through every type of love. A distinguishing feature of having a particularly evolved brain is not only our capacity to experience love, but to wield it in curious ways that may seem anathema to others. There are many ways to articulate our love, and there doesn't seem to be an act we aren't willing to commit in the name of it. We're honest and we lie out of love, liberate and enslave, support and deny, create and destroy, and we organize our entire lives around things we're gambling on being a valid interpretation of it. But how are we to know? And how are we to make sense of the acts committed in its name? It's all very strange, isn't it? What might an authentic representation of love look like? Are some of these acts committed by those confused about what love really is? I believe so.

Love is a concept so abstract that it remains impossible to define in a way that we would all accept, and I'm not going to try and define it in a way that addresses the totality of every dynamic present in every situation. Rather, I am going to try and give it *some* definition, so that we can more readily recognize if what we are seeing is in fact the authentic product. For a long time, I felt that love was best characterized not by any specific sort of exchange, but perhaps the exchange itself. A framework of pure reciprocity where despite what is given, it is always returned. It sounds nice, and it may certainly be a part of a healthy and happy relationship, but there are two flaws with it. The first is that this would only apply to relationships between equally capable adults, each in their own way. Love may be exchanged in every iteration of relationship, but nothing more than the affection itself can be reciprocated; a child cannot do for you what you do for them, neither can a pet, or abstractions like culture and God. The second is that reciprocity isn't a measure of authenticity, it is a mechanism for cohesion, so while it is valuable and I genuinely seek it out in all of my relationships, it does not permeate the categories in a useful manner to identify an archetype. An archetype needs to be a reliable framework that contains patterned truth that is authentic, identifiable, and useful.

Here we go.

The Floral Framework

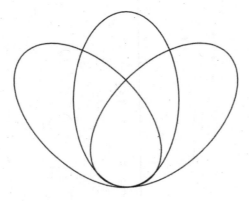

A framework is like an archetype, it is a system or thing used as an example to follow or imitate. This is the framework I've constructed, it is empty right now, and it will be filled as we progress, but I wanted to clarify what we're working with for anyone unfamiliar with such diagrams. It is a type of Venn diagram, which is a model comprised of individual phenomenon that are positioned in a way to generate overlapping portions that illustrate what is produced by the combination of two or more phenomena.

I am using three phenomena, and they have three overlapping areas that produce three relationships. They are petals, not circles, but the idea remains the same. Let's give it the *Marguerite* treatment and tear the petals apart, so we can more clearly identify that which comprises the framework. Here we have the three petals:

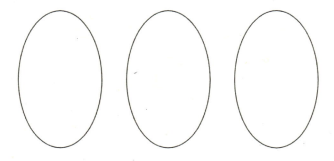

Not much to look at, so let's establish our phenomena, and relate them to the themes we've already covered in the book.

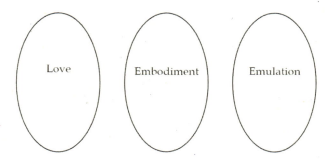

Now we have something to work with! Our three phenomena are love, embodiment, and emulation.

Love

Love is far too ambiguous and complicated to generalize and encapsulate in a single petal, but for our purposes, it will do. As I stated before, I am trying to tug at one of the threads of love to see if any sympathies are witnessed in the quilt. We don't all love the same, but we should be able to recognize which sorts of love produce results that we would typically associate with sabotage, or those what would more closely resemble being in the care of a dark heart, beating in the mist. My argument isn't that I possess the ability to define love, but I intend on clarifying some of the qualities of love. I am going to do this by examining various types of love and their inferences, and then to conclude which representations are authentic and therefore worthy of pursuing, and which are inauthentic, and should therefore be cautioned due to what they produce. I will make a thematic statement about love for the moment though: I believe that the essence of love is illustrated when we are seeking to improve someone or something for its own sake according to well-established wisdom.

Embodiment

To embody something is to be an expression of something in a visible form. We can embody many things, literally and figuratively, and when the expression is coherent, it is authentic. Authenticity and coherence in no way infer simplicity; an authentic expression is often multi-faceted and it may have components that may be fairly criticized as inauthentic, false, or performative. To a nuanced mind, this is obvious, and a tangible product with imperfect accessories is not rendered useless or worthless because it isn't pristine, because nothing is. The death of nuance is among the most prolific diseases of the modern era, and there doesn't seem to be an interest in flattening the curve. Simplistic and partisan narratives are readily espoused by the foolish and cocksure, who often jump at the opportunity to malign or dispense with any idea that they've identified possesses the taint of imperfection. Assertions made without evidence or wisdom have become the status quo, and when a deficit of self-awareness accompanies it, we should rightly be concerned.

Emulation

To emulate something is to imitate it. An emulation is a copy, a replica, or a shadow, it isn't the real thing. This is an important distinction, as even the best Elvis impersonator isn't Elvis himself; they behave in a performative way to cause you to perceive them as the authentic product. Emulations can very closely resemble an embodiment, and when we are the one converting thoughts and emotions into actions, we can't always accurately distinguish between them, especially when they *feel* the same. This is why my intention is to focus predominantly on the products of love, which will assist us in identifying if it's authentic or not, because our feelings and assumptions deceive us quite regularly. The deception is natural, and it often serves another purpose, a potentially valuable one at that, but that doesn't make it an authentic product of what we believe we are engaging with. Our brain is a much better lawyer than a judge, and we sooner find clever justifications prior to objective or reasoned perspectives, if we ever reach those at all.

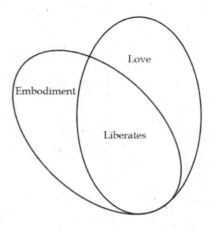

Authentic Love Liberates

Now that we've examined the individual petals, it's time to examine one of the overlaps. It is my belief that authentic representations of love, regardless of the context of care, liberate the affected and promote the opportunity to unlock potential. This overlap is a corollary of the Muses, who are the embodiment of inspiration, authentic and godly. If I have managed to avoid your condemnation so far, then this part and the next may attract some ire. Humans do not appreciate being labeled inauthentic or wrong, but even if you disagree, perhaps it will inspire a desire to discuss such concepts and their potential value with your friends and relatives.

I mentioned a few contexts earlier wherein love is often present as a human experience, according to the minds and mouths of many. For clarity of my argument, I think it is important to distinguish between two pretenses that may both be occurring at any given time where love is present: relationships defined by care, and individual acts of care. The dynamics of a relationship shift over time and recognizing the interplay of love and circumstance will offer insight into distinguishing between authentic and inauthentic representations of love. Let's keep these in mind as we examine the first overlap.

When you're in a relationship defined by care, there are expectations that establish responsibilities for the parties that are capable of demonstrating care. There is nothing wrong with this, as a commitment to someone often infers some amount of dedication in caring for them, although this will look different for every relationship. The capability of someone is a measure of their capacity to distinguish between authentic and inauthentic love, keeping in mind that we are differentiating them based on what they produce. A partner or spouse are equally capable of an authentic mutual exchange of love as they are both in a position to engage in relational care, and to examine their respective outcomes. Additionally, they are both equally capable of performing individual acts of care that are done for a litany of reasons, but still fall within the framework. Siblings, friends, and your fellow citizens are similar in this regard, provided they are adults. The reason for this is because we can all engage with one another in a manner that liberates us and provides us with an opportunity to unlock potential. We can all engage in reciprocal exchanges of care that may consist of teaching, learning, lifting a burden, cooperation, and consolation that generate opportunities to unlock potential through reflection, introspection, skill development, and obtaining knowledge, or through the effective grappling of the tension embedded in the situation within which we receive assistance.

Individual acts of care are done beyond a sense of commitment or obligation, but they can prove just as authentic in the realm of love. Doing something for another either alleviates them of a specific burden like a chore, or maintains a commitment. If you alleviate a burden, you free them to tackle another burden of potentially greater value, which will yield a far greater unlocking of potential. It can also be done to permit another to rest, weary from an existence defined by challenges and riddled with stress, so that they can recuperate and be much more well-positioned to meet existing and future challenges. Commitments require maintenance, and doing regular maintenance on anything generally tends to keep it in better working order. Complications that arise in the realm of commitment are often due to an inability to recognize the value of the person or the thing being maintained, which could be an accurate depiction of its poor quality, or a shortcoming, depending on the situation.

The relationship between parents and children are also defined by a commitment of care, but the dynamic is completely different. Most parents love their children, but this doesn't mean that all acts of care are authentic depictions of love. Children are in a unique position relative to their parents, one of dependence. Parents should ideally be sufficiently present in their children's lives to assist in moderating existence in an effort to produce someone competent. Parents are the default devourers, and it should be easy to see how they can consume their child's competence through inauthentic representations of love; this will be covered in greater detail in the next parts. Parents can also be placed in a position of dependence relative to their children, and this occurs with far greater frequency than I would've anticipated in my youth. Alzheimer's and dementia are complicated and debilitating conditions that rob the sufferers of their identities and burden relatives, typically their children, with managing an impossible series of dilemmas that occur in a never-ending sequence. That being said, it is important for the health of all parties involved that you never do anything for them that they can do for themselves, which is sound advice for children as well.

This exchange of dependence roles permits children to see the importance of independence from a vantage point that would've been otherwise unattainable. Those who suffer with severe mental impairments in their old age often demand to be left alone, and to interfere with whatever remaining capacity they possess to do some things for themselves is perceived as an insult to their dignity. This is because they aren't children, and as such, they have learned throughout their lives that the dignity we obtain through self-care and competence is part of what comprises the identity of a human worthy of living. Children have yet to learn this, which is what makes them easy targets for institutional devourers like school, religion, and government, which leap at opportunities to comfort and console in the pursuit of adherence through the consumption of their competence.

Pets are a peculiar case, but they are strangely simple to frame. We all have relationships with our pets defined by care, but they have far less ambiguous limitations on their ceilings of competence due to their neurobiology and general intelligence. Pets aren't stupid, far from it, but they are nowhere near as smart as a child, and many animals simply don't possess a sufficiently advanced brain to contend with the sort of potential that a human can unlock. Opposable thumbs help too. Despite these limitations, we can do many things that demonstrate authentic love to provide them with the best opportunities to live a life with as few obstacles as possible. We can make sure their diet is adequate to improve overall health and longevity, and provide suitable exercise for the same reason. We can provide them with challenges and games that assist them in developing skills for problem solving, or train them to perform actions uncommon to a basic existence. We can make sure they have a schedule that they can recognize and rely upon in order to maintain a stable existence. We can groom them and develop trust, and demonstrate care for them that many pets intuitively recognize. We can also care for them inauthentically, which will be addressed shortly.

Love for your country or culture is difficult to pin down, because they aren't recipients of care in any coherent way. *Country* could be a stand-in for citizenry, which contains some coherence of concept, and it could also be a proxy for *government*, which is certainly an entity, but it is more clearly characterized as an established set of functions rather than a personification of one sort or another. Culture is the residue of knowledge and wisdom that is contextually correct for the paradigm within which it functions, and although you may be proud to be part of one culture or another, you are merely congratulating yourself on your fortune. You cannot care for it, and it cannot receive it, and attempts at trying to establish coherence in this relationship will cause a feedback loop to emerge with you as both the giver and receiver.

A government can care for its people, even authentically, by removing barriers that interfere with the individual pursuit of meaning and unlocking of potential. An individual caring for the government is grotesque. You can respect the government, recognize the need for it, cooperate with it, and rely on its monopoly on violence provided it isn't corrupt, but it is a parasite by definition. If government funding is functioning correctly, it is an immortal leech, consuming a portion of your livelihood, and the size of its meal increases incrementally over time, as self-perpetuating systems do. I am not anti-government, but caution must be at the forefront of our minds when considering the extent to which any entity will seek to remove obstacles that impede its own evolution, especially when ethics and accountability are deliberately side-stepped, fundamentally misunderstood, or non-existent.

An individual that has love for the government likely needs more religion in their life, if only to be confronted with the dangers of improper worship. A relationship with one or more gods can be orienting, and it may produce liberation, but the dynamics of this are incredibly complicated. Often an entirely new equilibrium extends from this relationship where we commit to a relationship defined by care with a personified idea that both burdens us with expectations and provides us with continuity, and this may produce liberation of many sorts. These relationships may not be *real* in the traditional sense, but it is difficult to deny their truth, or perhaps, their meta-truth. For now, I will say that I remain skeptical about the authenticity of any representations of love in a relationship with God within my framework, but that I recognize the value of such relationships outside the confines of this concept.

We can frequently define things rather easily based on observable phenomena, but often it is only after examining the tension that emerges after injecting its opposite into the argument that the picture becomes clear. Let's do that now.

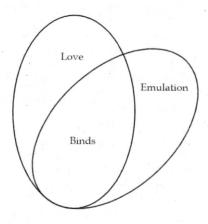

Inauthentic Love Binds

The second overlap, and the more critical one, is what is produced when an inauthentic, or emulated, representation of love is at play. It is my belief that inauthentic representations of love, within the aforementioned contexts, bind the affected and tether them to an ideal or person, which will interfere with opportunities to unlock their potential. This overlap is a corollary of the Sirens, who are the embodiment of captivating comfort, inauthentic and twisted. The binding nature of emulated love, done at the expense of the affected, and serving at the pleasure of the giver, is a foundational component of the devouring mother, of which Medusa is an example.

Generally speaking, inauthentic love is a far greater concern in relationships defined by care, as opposed to individual acts of care; however, individual acts done over time, even in the absence of an established relationship defined by care, can have the same effect. With regards to spouses and their accompanying adult siblings, friends, and fellow citizens, much can be done to bind us in place, fat and comfortable while we remain malnourished and stable. An important thing to mention here is that inauthentic acts of care may be inconsequential within a larger context of relational care that contains a preponderance of authentic care; an equilibrium can be maintained even with inauthentic representations of love, and inauthentic acts of care can be done by otherwise authentic individuals. The purpose of this framework is to assist us in distinguishing between the masks in our old dusty bin, not to insinuate that any of us are capable of avoiding any particular mask indefinitely. Observations that can assist us with this are the presence of reciprocal authenticity and the capabilities of the recipient.

Is the person to whom you're directing your care capable of reciprocating? Are they willing to reciprocate? One is a question of competence, the other, morality. Additionally, are the affected interested in your care? Doing something for someone is generally considered a positive thing, but this is a dramatic oversimplification of the twisted human web of motivations, incentives, mechanisms, goals, and approvals. There are a series of very important questions that should be considered if we're serious about distinguishing between authentic and inauthentic representations of love. I'm going to hit you with a bunch now, it's hammer time.

Why am I doing what I'm doing? Why have I specifically chosen this particular act of care? What does this choice say about me? Why do I believe it is better to do this rather than not? What is the value of this act? What is the value of alternative acts of care? What is the value of abstaining all together? What are the externalities that may be acting upon my decision-making that cause me to experience doubt or validation? To what extent are these reasonable or fair?

What am I gaining from this act of care? What is the recipient gaining? Is my experience in performing this act consoling for me? If so, why? Is the act consoling for the recipient? If so, what are the short-term benefits? What are the long-term effects on the recipient if acts of this sort become commonplace? Do I possess the knowledge to discover these answers? Do I possess the wisdom and modesty to recognize if my conclusions are well-founded, and not machinations or justifications?

Am I demonstrating my care in an effective manner? Is it authentic? Does it authentically represent my intentions and desired outcomes? Am I aware of any peripheral ethical dilemmas that accompany my actions? Do I possess the requisite faculties to navigate these ethical dilemmas effectively and minimize inauthentic products? Have I experienced or observed similar acts of care and compared them to my own in a critical and honest manner? To what extent am I injecting my own bias into the mechanism of the act? Is this useful or damaging for the recipient? Am I modest enough to recognize and acknowledge my own bias?

Am I aware of my goal? Am I able to identify the potential effects of my actions on the recipient? Is my goal coherent? Am I able to identify whether or not my actions contribute to my goal? If my goal is achieved, who benefits? How do they benefit? If multiple people benefit, am I able to parse their respective qualities in order to determine their authenticity? Is it common for me to engage in post-hoc reasoning or justification in order to preserve my ego? Am I doing this now?

Then there is the matter of approval. Does the recipient approve of my act? Did they request it? Are they capable of refusing it? Do they agree with the assessment I've made about my actions? If they disagree, to what extent am I willing to consider myself more knowledgeable about their conscious experience than they are? If I am, what does this say about me? How certain am I about the recipient's desire or need for my act? Did I discuss it with them? If the need is authentic, where is it located in a hierarchy of their needs? How did I identify their needs in the first place? Is it generalizable? Does this affect the validity or authenticity of my goal?

That's a lot of questions, and it isn't likely that anyone would be willing to consider all of them in any given endeavour, that would take a lot of time! But we can select a few, ones that we've identified are helpful in keeping us on the right track, once we've come to terms with our own susceptibilities.

Activism is an interesting phenomenon in this case, because the legitimacy of it can often be easily recognized based on the motivations of the activist, in whose interest it is being done, and the degree of consensus and complicity inherent in the stakeholder population. Most of modern activism in the Western world has become a scam, with self-interested and particularly noisy individuals speaking on behalf on huge swaths of people, often deliberately categorized in ambiguous and general ways, without any concern for precisely how much of any population they genuinely represent, and always without election. I've yet to hear any apprehension or doubt from the mouths of modern activists about the validity or necessity of their goals, or even a modicum of modesty that they don't represent nearly as many people as they would purport to. A movement without an appreciation for honesty or modesty is a scam, especially when time may be better spent investing locally in a community to lift up one another, rather than tear down civilization based on obviously stupid reasoning. If an act of care is done in the interest of liberating someone to the extent that they can unlock potential, then it can be authentic, but any act that tethers someone to an ambiguous cause or binds others in place to serve as bystanders is inauthentic and fueled by resentment.

Relationships defined by care between consenting adults will have their fair share of complexities, but when the vulnerable are involved, like children for instance, who are dependent on the care of their parents or teachers and cannot opt out so easily, deliberate or inadvertent care that can bind takes on a far more nefarious persona.

There is a common glazing over of the details of a particular task that results in a parent or teacher intervening to complete a task that could otherwise be completed by someone in their care. Are they able to do this task themselves? If so, then let them do it, and if they do it poorly, guide them on how to do it better. If they can't do it, then can they at least do part of it? If so, then let them do that part, and show them how the various parts connect. If they can't do any part of it, teach it to them. Is it easier to just do it for them? Perhaps, and it may be equally parts more efficient and sanity-retaining depending on the circumstance to be sure, but who is this for? Caring parents will state that it is being done for the child, and this may true, but even so, it is only ever true in one way. It is also true that insisting that they problem-solve the task themselves is also being done for the child, it just doesn't present quite as caring at the time.

A shortcut for most acts of care directed towards a child is short-term versus long-term benefit. Generally speaking, authentic love will likely generate temporary or short-term stress or delay, but it creates the opportunity for potential to be realized and then unlocked, which benefits them in the long term. On the other hand, inauthentic love will generate temporary or short-term gratification and comfort, but it sabotages the child from developing competence by interfering in the natural process of learning, and it will generate suffering in the long term; they'll be set adrift on the seas, ready to be caught in the lure of a siren's song. Without developing the competence and self-respect necessary to recognize and grapple with truth and meaning, how will they find a way to reliably ease their existential dread and become a being worthy of the life they've been given? This isn't a small matter; it can often pose as the main obstacle to happiness and contentment.

I deliberately constructed this elaboration to be absent any specificity; I'm sure you're able to interpret the point of the example and apply it in whichever way you choose. I am not seeking enemies through direct attacks on parenting or teaching methods, none of us are perfect, I just wanted to produce something that can be grappled with. Pets are much simpler, and I'll move on from children to save both of us from the tension of the conversation. Essentially, do your actions make your pet more dependent on you? Or less? Are they a companion or your toy? Did you get your particular pet precisely because they would be more dependent on you than another would be? What does that say about you? Would you be afraid if people knew the reason? Are you ashamed of the reason? Do you know that what you're doing is inhibiting to their independence? Do you mind? If not, why not?

A government that makes itself needlessly necessary in your life is the devouring mother writ large. A government is likely necessary for numerous legitimate processes in a democratic and free society, and engaging in these processes so that you can improve your life on your own terms is sufficient enough to qualify as authentic care. A government that generates redundant or inhibitory processes for no discernable reason other than for bureaucratic proliferation or revenue generation is not a government, it's your boss, and a boss that also has a monopoly on violence is incapable of authentic care. A dynamic like this perpetuates a system where you serve at the pleasure of the government, and not the other way around, as it should be.

Being selected as a representative is an honour that is defined and justified solely on the assumption that you serve at the pleasure of your constituents, not that you are wiser than them, more capable, or more important. You are a voice with a mind that is expected to wield the authority and influence granted to you by virtue of your office in a manner that is concordant with the expectations and desires of the citizenry. They're busy making everything work and trying to live their lives to the best of their ability, and the purpose of a politician is to grease the wheels of social progress according to the interests of those that actually make things work. Politicians often become confused about this, and they confuse honour with self-importance, and influence with unfettered power, to be exercised as they see fit, presumably because they believe they know what's best for you; you're clueless, that's why you need them, right? A government or representative that acts as merely an emulation of love will seek to make you dependant on them and all of their inadequacies while attempting to convince you that you need them, whether you like it or not.

An examination of inauthentic love in a relationship with God could be exhaustively long and dicey; fortunately, I have something relatively succinct to say about this. If your relationship with God inspires you and brings out the best in you in a way that you find comfort and a healthy and cohesive attitude towards your fellow humans, then this would constitute authentic love. If it binds you, limits you, generates a sense of unease, or compels you to establish or retain a divisive attitude towards your fellow humans that is antithetical to reciprocity and truth, then it is false. If it's the latter, find another God or worship another way. I will leave that to your discretion.

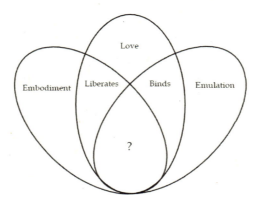

There is a matter left unresolved, which is what emerges in the tension where both authentic and inauthentic love are present. Certainly, a balance can be struck, as a sign of extremism in most cases would generally constitute pathology or tyranny. Is there a place for this tension? What does it look like? Is it valuable? Yes, of course, and in most situations, it is a necessary predicate to intermittently guide both the giver and the recipient towards being liberated or bound, and assist us in recognizing useful configurations that will ultimately shape how we perceive our own existence.

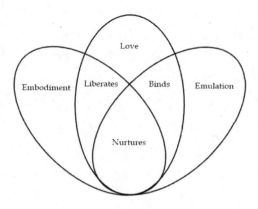

Nurturing Tension

A balance that has been struck between embodied and emulated love nurtures the recipient, and if we're doing it properly, it nurtures the giver as well. Intermittent nurturing is useful, grounding, and cohesive for everyone. The degree of its stability will depend on how well-tuned the stakeholders are in cooperating honestly during exchanges. It is also useful for orienting, regardless of which position we are in. If we find ourselves consuming competence through care, and binding the recipient in place, we can swing back towards the centre like a pendulum, and reassess our conduct. On the contrary, if we find ourselves making unreasonable demands on a predominantly liberated recipient who has yet to develop competence, then we may need to reassess our conduct in order to manage the expectations we've imposed. The intention here isn't to liberate the bound and bind the liberated. Rather, we should seek to restore a sense of equilibrium and create the tension that will generate a competent individual. The recognition of this is only possible if we possess the capacity to doubt ourselves.

To nurture someone is to care for them while encouraging growth. Growth, in this instance, is not meant to describe the development of an increasingly resilient bond, it describes the development of an increasingly resilient individual. Care can be binding in a very important way in certain circumstances, and dependants like children need boundaries and limitations that assist in socializing them, even if we believe that aspects of the broader context are antithetical to human health and flourishing. We need to learn how to get along with a world comprised of humans possessing a nearly infinite number of individual configurations. To insist on an existence completely unfettered by some number of boundaries will likely generate unnecessary conflict and ego. We need to sacrifice part of our potential in order to socialize properly, and we are all expected to do this because it's a good deal; what we receive in return through reciprocity of similar actors will constitute a far greater number of authentic exchanges of care that would've been incapable of materializing in the absence of such a sacrifice.

A state of constant nurturing is possible for anyone, regardless of age, and we would serve ourselves well to surround ourselves with those that keep us in check, but that also bring out the best in us. We can have our moments of perfectly acceptable liberation while in pursuit of a goal, and this is how great things that we all benefit from come to be. At some point though, we need to re-examine the status of our position, and determine if we're on the right track; this is discipline. A disciplined person can still benefit from care, but they engage in a healthy amount of authentic self-care that, when guided by truth, honesty, and ethics, will create an ecosystem within an individual that self-iterates and improves on itself not only so that they can keep themselves oriented, but also to help others orient themselves. More concisely: nurturing begets competence, competence begets responsibility, responsibility begets discipline, and discipline begets the confidence to realize the limits of our potential on our own terms. From there, we can still go an infinite number of directions, and the ego and ethics are still up for grabs, but it's the foundation upon which we are given the opportunity to live a life worth living, instead of one defined by servitude.

Flowers of Flesh and Blood

To round off the framework, I'd like to make an analogy. It is often up to fortune whether we are the one tearing the petals one by one, or the target of the affection. It is another matter entirely to take on the characteristics of the flower, and serve as the mechanism through which fate is decided. Would you rule authentically? Or would you be a reflection; merely an emulation? If given the chance to act as the intermediary of fortune between two or more people, what would your qualities and characteristics be? Would you liberate or bind? What sort of people do you find yourself surrounded by? What sort of person would you want someone in your care to become? What sort of flower would they be? What sort of flower are you?

Despite any misleading advertising or shallow placative self-help books, loving yourself isn't a virtue, in fact, it's likely to cause you harm. Identifying and acknowledging the authentic parts of yourself, all of the good and bad, improving your shortcomings that can be improved, playing to your strengths, and accepting the totality of your being is a much better strategy, and it's less likely to make you insufferable to others. Although I don't believe in original sin, virtually all of us are a mess in one way or another, so I'm not sure why encouraging others to love what might be a broken or lost soul is supposed to be valuable beyond any temporary therapeutic relief it offers; it's a bad strategy. People are real, and we need something real to orient us, or you may end up as a daffodil.

Narcissus, a character from Greek mythology, is also the name of a flower. Narcissus is part of the amaryllis family, and it is a type of daffodil. For those unfamiliar, in the myth, Narcissus, a hunter who was renowned for his beauty, rejected all romantic advances, and he eventually fell in love with his own reflection in a pool of water. He stared at it for the remainder of his life, and although this isn't explicitly stated, he likely starved to death. At the location of his death, a daffodil sprouted, and it was subsequently named after him, or so the story goes. Whether this flower was a daffodil is debatable, but it's also immaterial.

A hunter needs to *hunt*, and a human needs to *human*, and to sit idly, enamoured with our own existence is antithetical to both. The ironic part of the myth is that Narcissus is a hunter, but failed to successfully capture a lover, and in the end failed miserably to be an effective one, instead falling in love with his own reflection. He didn't love anything that he hunted or earned, only that which was given to him by the circumstances of his beauty, his own shadow. This myth illustrates a coalescence of numerous deadly sins, which is helpful in understanding why it may be resonant. Narcissus becomes a glutton when sees himself and he fawns over his own reflection, but it doesn't nourish or nurture, and so he starves. He greedily keeps his care to himself, refusing all romantic advances, unwilling to take a chance or share a part of himself with others. He embodies sloth, and rests indefinitely until he dies due to the comfort of his stasis. You could make the case for lust, but it doesn't really fit too well. Wrath, envy, and pride aren't particularly coherent in any meaningful way, but there might be an overly enthusiastic individual out there that may try and psychoanalyze a character from Greek mythology, not that I would ever do anything like that.

Medusa and other devouring mothers would approve of Narcissus. What is produced by her can be likened to Narcissus, an entity who believes themselves excellent and worthwhile merely by existing and not through accomplishment, and they will waste away, gazing at their own reflection. This concept is reinforced by the fact that they perceive the devouring mother to serve at their pleasure, worship them, and whose existence appears to be solely predicated on comforting them. Humans are comprised mostly of water, and although it isn't likely that the ancient Greeks knew this, it is cute that the reflection with which he fell in love was found in water, not a mirror or another surface. He gazes upon that which comprises himself and falls in love, sort of like seeing ourselves on social media.

A devouring mother will plant daffodil seeds, but do they even like daffodils? Do they even know what they're planting? What else could someone plant, if they didn't want daffodils? They could plant jasmine, which is one of the nicest smelling flowers, but it is notoriously delicate. A rose is frequently considered the nicest smelling flower, and it is a bit more resilient than jasmine. Snapdragons are very colourful and highly resilient, and chocolate cosmos have a sweet, sugary smell, a unique colour, and a velvety texture. A sunflower is among the tallest flowers, and it is one of many examples of the golden ratio found in nature, enigmatic and symmetrical in design. A daylily is a very resilient and colourful flower, and it is known to attract hummingbirds and butterflies, a welcome addition to any garden. These all have their respective worth, and we can plant various seeds in a garden in an attempt to have a more complete bouquet.

Then there are some flowers we'd likely deem unwelcome in our gardens. A rafflesia is the largest flower on Earth, but having the biggest bloom isn't all it's cracked up to be. It emits a repulsive odour to attract insects, not for pollination, but to consume them. It is a predatory plant with no visible leaves, roots or stems. It attaches itself to a host plant to obtain water and nutrients, so it can dine on insects that are lured by its foul nature; a rafflesia is the psychopath of flowers. Another one worth avoiding would be a corpse flower, which is among the largest flowers, but it's not technically a single flower. It is a cluster of many tiny flowers, called an inflorescence, and it smells like rotting flesh. It's incredible what a small cluster of ineffectual flowers can produce when they team up.

Do you know which seeds you're planting? Do parents? Do friends and family? Do governments? The broader the scope of influence, the greater the concern for an ethical garden. Do we know how these flowers interact with one another? How much maintenance do they each require? How welcome is each one in a household? Or a schoolyard? What about a workplace? The head of a religion? The leader of a nation? I'll leave that to you.

You could argue that this book is unnecessary, because a proverb already exists claiming that *if you give a man a fish, you feed him for a day, and if you teach a man to fish, you feed him for a lifetime,* and this echoes with a similar lesson. If you believe such a thing to be true, however, do you know why you think it's true? Why do people believe that there is wisdom to be found in such a proverb? Or proverbs at all? What if you're a fisherman and you want to sell your fish? If you teach another to fish, then they may not buy your fish!

Perhaps, but it could also be that competition will make both of you better, and there will never be a shortage of people who need to eat, but will lack the ability and desire to fish for themselves. Not everyone needs to know how to fish, but they need to learn how to do *something and be good at it*, and this requires competence which can only be obtained if we aren't consumed by the maw of the mother. With this book, I am simply offering a glimpse into a *why* that may have previously eluded you. Once you learn *why* something is true, it becomes easier to see why other things may be true, and why some things are false. Valuable lessons don't merely teach, they provide, like a fisherman does for himself, and with the right set of lessons, we obtain something that serves us well in every endeavour: perspective.

In closing, I want to reiterate that although I have made my opinions known throughout this book, my intention isn't to tell you how to live your life. That being said, there are things that we've come to learn after hundreds of years about the nature of humans, and which strategies tend to produce the greatest likelihoods of prosperity and happiness. As a result, my goal is to try and share wisdom that I believe may be useful or helpful in figuring how to best live our lives in a manner that prioritizes human autonomy while respecting the broader social context. If you have found anything in this book interesting, then it has served its purpose. While some conclusions were offered, many more questions were left unanswered. This was done deliberately because these questions aren't for me to answer on your behalf. If I did, it simply wouldn't stick. People need to figure out these answers for themselves in order for them to integrate them effectively into their lives. This is a universal truth. If I pretended to have all of the answers, or give you more than you need to get started, then I'm no different than the litany of people I've criticized throughout this book that parasitize others for their own purposes.

You are a human of flesh and blood that breathes and lives, and I believe it is unethical to try and program you as if you were merely a construct of solder and wire, executing the software I've written.

None of us asked to be born, but despite any challenges or suffering that plague us, it is still an opportunity to experience a life that could've just as easily never have been offered. Knowing ourselves is a moral imperative, and recognizing what we are, what works and does not, and respecting the accumulation of knowledge that has brought us to where we are is necessary if we are to orient ourselves towards something worthy of our existence. Always be honest, and be pleasant when you can, but remain fearless in the face of those that seek to interfere with your capacity to develop the wisdom required to make informed decisions that will dictate the state of your conscience. To examine your life from the apex of old age and regret a past that you can no longer change is among the worst experiences we can have. Do your best to avoid this and assist others in doing the same. Truth is one of the most potent catalysts for accumulating meaning, and our spirits will wander aimlessly in the absence of its orienting power.

Viciously pursue truth with courage and kindness, because if you're owed anything by virtue of your birth, it is the opportunity to pursue an existence that is more than just breathing.

ACKNOWLEDGMENTS

Nothing is ever accomplished solely through the thoughts or actions of a single person, and I'd like to thank those that helped me along the way.

With regards to content, I'd like to thank Benjamin Khan for assisting me in producing a much higher-resolution breakdown of the Floral Framework, and to Tara Alexander, whose correspondence served as an excellent introduction to the concept of truth as a pattern. Thank you to Jon D'Orazio for the awesome drawing of the multi-tool in this book, and the logos for my podcast and shirts, and to Tobias "Cheetah" Schnitzhofer for making the music and background for my podcast, and who engages regularly in the comments on my videos. I'd like to thank Shannon Alexander for reviewing my manuscript and providing valuable feedback that caused me to re-write certain parts for both clarity and accessibility. Thank you to Rosemary Gonzales and Dan Reid, whom I tortured for two years during scheduled breaks and lunches at work with discussions about my thoughts when I'm sure they would've much rather done anything else. Thank you to Meaghan Martinho for being one of my biggest supporters, and from very early on encouraging me to move on to bigger and better things because I am wasted potential at work. Lastly, I'd like to thank Derek Peterson for being interesting and tall, not boring and smol.

I wrote the vast majority of this book enjoying a drink at Ivy Arms in Milton, Ontario, and in the absence of this welcoming establishment, this book would never have been written. I'd like to thank the staff for always being supportive and for assisting in my escape.

ABOUT THE AUTHOR

MATTHEW ANGHELOS MARCH is a philosopher in the pursuit of helping humanity. With a focus on logic, ethics, and epistemology, he attempts to provide useful perspectives that anyone can adopt to find meaning in their life, and ultimately, truth. He hosts a philosophy podcast that promotes critical thinking and honest discussion. Though he once planned to become a vigilante, he now works to redeem himself as an instructor for the federal government, delivering a variety of material including mental health courses designed to help officers reduce workplace stress and PTSD. He has a keen interest in the welfare of others, and is always seeking to develop his understanding of human nature and the human condition. He lives in Milton, Ontario, with his books.

Printed in Canada